Pe

By Samantha

Permission To Be Myself
ISBN: 978-1-9161700-1-8

First published in Great Britain
in 2019 through Amazon self-publishing
service Kindle Direct Publishing

Disclaimer: real names/places
have been changed to protect the identities.

Produced by samanthahoughton.co.uk

Dedication

To every person in this life that struggles to be themselves. I know your pain. It is often our self that is not allowing that so I urge you to read on and to honour yourself that permission and to be free.

To my loving son, Joe.

Words from Joe

When my mum said she was writing her second book and a considerable section focussed on me and my struggles I was a bit unsure at first. Although, after a bit of thought, I was on board with the idea. Firstly, I understand how writing helps her to release and gain clarity on her struggles. Without writing honestly about me, this would have felt incomplete and inaccurate. But also, having personally reflected on my struggles, I realised that despite having endured some very difficult times, I had nothing to be ashamed about. I feel no reason to hide what I have felt, many people suffer from anxiety, even if they don't actively speak about it. Hopefully, sharing this story will help others in a similar position, who may feel trapped and scared about those problems, especially those who don't have someone as supportive as my mum, who helped me immeasurably throughout, even if she hasn't always thought that of herself.

Author Bio

Samantha Houghton lives in Leicester in the UK and is mum to Joe. This is her second book authored in her name, she also has written several other books as a ghost-writer and recently created a compilation of true mental health stories. She also works in her business as a book mentor with her life's purpose to support others to write and publish their true-life stories and self-help books as she firmly believes that it is inspirational stories that connect us and that make a difference to humanity. She specialises in mental health and trauma relating to her background and shares a great passion and understanding of this along with living as a highly sensitive person.

Contents

1. The Aftermath 9
2. Making It Happen 13
3. Cabbaged Head 15
4. My Thing 18
5. The Invisible Girl 21
6. The Launch 23
7. The Book Tour 26
8. A New Diagnosis? 30
9. A New Purpose 34
10. University Abound 37
11. An Award and a Night At St Pancras Station 42
12. Design Your Life 49
13. Collaboration 53
14. Manifestation 56
15. Exorcising Ghosts 59
16. The Summer of 2018 63
17. Don't Do Things By Halves 70
18. Black Christmas 73
19. A Christmas Like No Other 80
20. Boxing Day 84
21. The End 87
22. The Word Was Epic 90
23. Courage: Stories Of Darkness To Light 95
24. The Good, The Bad and The Ugly 98
25. Magic 105
26. Flipping Out of Abundance 107
27. Escape To The Sea 112
28. Returning to Normality 118
29. CEO Of Your Life 121

Other Books and Contact info 124

1

The Aftermath

"You needed therapy every two to three years of your adult life Sam – what the hell was wrong with you?" These harsh words screamed out at me and the intense secretive shame consumed me immediately followed by tears.

After writing my first book, I was both delighted and exhausted. It was quite an intense, emotional journey in a short space of time, sixteen days to be exact as my soul had guided me to spill my truth. Reflecting on my forty six years and bringing it to life on the pages brought up a lot of *"stuff"*.

I remembered things that I didn't realise I could remember and I felt the emotions almost as rawly as I did at the time as I dived deep into my memories to portray my story the best I could tell it some thirty years later. Seeing it all through adult eyes gave me many different perspectives that caused my mind to spin. One aspect really jumped out at me though, more than anything else; and that was how I saw a pattern of needing to reach out for help every two to three years. I drew up a simple diagram of my therapy time-line and it shocked me. Even though I knew this had happened, seeing it as obviously as this sketch greatly upset me.

Since 1985, I had been admitted as an in-patient in a psychiatric setting four times. I had received the following therapies over the thirty two year span (that I can recall):

Psychiatrist consultations, occupational therapy, group psychotherapy, family therapy, psychodrama, eating disorder therapy, psycho-dynamic psychotherapy, community psychiatric nursing, person centred counselling, psycho-dynamic counselling, CBT, solution focussed therapy, mentoring, life coaching, relationship counselling and inter personal psychotherapy.

Plus the medications: many different anti –depressants and tranquillisers, anti-psychotics and short term use of sleeping tablets. Yet, despite all this *'help'*, I still had struggled. I had been on auto pilot, thinking, but not *'seeing'* the bigger picture. I went back for help each time but never really questioned a professional medical person why, and why I was not better.

In between my dips and treatments, I was furiously working on my self-development in isolation - particularly during the last decade. Pushing myself forwards, literally having to dare myself with most of the steps that I took. It felt to me, seeing things from the perspective of the former person I was, who was afraid of nearly everything, that this took a tremendous amount of courage. Reading my own story shocked me because of how much of a struggle my life had been. I am still convinced it is not meant to be this way for anyone. We are born to feel joy and peace, otherwise, why would we be here?

I began to do some intensive research and reading other people's books. I had my own suspicions and had considered my thoughts about my latest realisation a few years ago, but a big part of me did not want to go back and delve anymore. However, fast forward a few years and that unresolved stuff comes back with a vengeance. You can only keep issues down for so long before they reappear and rear their ugly head. Now the time felt right. I had found the courage to reveal a lot of my inner thoughts and experiences with the universe through my book so I was in a daring mood. There was no reason to hide anymore.

One book that I read, the majority of it within two days

as I couldn't put it down, had some influence on my life. It was as though this female author, of her memoir, had got into my head and it was like reading about myself. Different characters, some different experiences, but the thoughts, thought processes, struggles, painful overbearing emotions were written as I felt them and I could deeply identify with them; Incredible. I felt a relief as this felt like a mammoth confirmation and validation of my lingering what ifs and unanswered questions. I felt as though I knew this author as we had shared so much just through the pages. She was an amazing lady and I really had an ache that I wanted to meet her one day to thank her.

I then began to read as much as I could on the subject and as in my usual style, became mildly, ahem, obsessed. More reading later, and I felt ever more validation and decided I wanted a professional opinion: - Not to live under a label, as I knew first hand how damaging these could be, but for peace of mind. I think part of me wanted the medical professionals to recognise both this awakening I'd reached, and the struggle it had been to get there. This was vastly due to some of the most invalidating feelings I'd experienced originating from professionals. Within a fortnight I had an appointment booked to see my G.P. It was not going to be easy in trying to explain to him, so I wrote some pointers down.

In the meantime, some pretty amazing happenings had occurred in relation to my book. My close friend Gill, had expressed an interest in reading some of it as no one had set eyes on it as yet. After meeting for coffee one Saturday afternoon in a cosy village café, I got home and emailed her some chapters across. My book was currently in a word document, all forty seven thousand words wrapped up in twenty seven chapters. Later that evening, she replied and said that she loved reading what I had sent her and could she please read the rest. I shrieked in delight and eagerly agreed. Even though I had known her for many years and we had been through a lot together, it was still daunting for someone else to read my personal writings for the first time. This was very encouraging.

I woke up in the middle of that night feeling very sick and with grappling stomach pains, which fast progressed into a nasty stomach bug.

2

Making It Happen

As ill as I felt that Sunday morning, reading Gill's email telling me how much she loved my book and that she had stayed up very late to read it, really brightened me up and added onto the confidence I was feeling about making this a reality.

I felt really rough for almost a week, and I felt low being inactive, which gave me too much time to think. I was cross, as I had to miss a talk I was giving at Leicester University about my story. I improved at the end of the week, and started to plan on my next stage with getting my book to become published and an actual book you could hold in your hand. A moment I had dreamed of, for years, being able to sign my physical book for new readers: - You know, one of those random dreams you have that never fail to inspire you. I researched and got some advice; one lady gave me the idea of using a Crowd-funding platform for a book such as mine as she had done for her book. It sounded like a great idea, especially as all of my money had gone into a course on how to create online courses.

I set up my project and within a week so many amazing happenings occurred, it will go down as one of the best weeks ever, the Law of Attraction was playing in my favour most definitely. I began to get contributions flooding in, then people came forward to help me with design, proof reading and photography. To end the week on a high, I was granted the opportunity to have my book launch at a local event about six weeks away that supported disabilities - it would be perfect. I was truly amazed at people's kindness. I was texting and ringing my mum frequently that week, squealing with delight and gratitude and I wanted her to share my excitement. The pre – publishing stage began to take shape.

Meanwhile I went to see my GP. I asked for a referral for some specific therapy for what I believed to have been my long term issue after all of this time and I was convinced that I still had remnants of this to deal with. He listened to me as I got very upset sharing my thoughts. He agreed with me and referred me onwards. He was very kind.

I continued to feel very mixed up as everything was taking time to process and I kept having *"a – ha"* moments, with more questions being raised, or things falling into place. I also started to have very vivid and often disturbing dreams at night and my usual good night's sleep became interrupted.

All of this was interspersed with sad moments of thinking about Joe leaving in a few months time and of my imminent life change when he left, including my career and financial situation; it was a very difficult time. I kept reminding myself that I had been through far worse but it didn't really relieve those dark few weeks. It was ironic really that I was back in touch with Vicki and another person from Chester Lodge, the psychiatric unit I'd been admitted to for 16 months of my teen years.

3

Cabbaged Head

As I sat, on a Saturday morning, in a bustling café, I didn't even feel real. I believe this was a form of dissociation. It is hard to describe what was happening to me. I felt like the life I had built and known was crumbling down and I was really scared. I have a love/hate relationship with the unknown (not an easy choice to be a business owner!) and it all felt very unknown at this moment in time. As I think back to the emotions I was feeling, it's all I could do to stop the tears from falling as I was trembling inside. I felt so vulnerable, wanting to burst into tears; feeling strange and lost, so I pulled out my note pad and began to write instead. Confused would not come close to how I was feeling right then.

All I had known, the major parts of my life for the past eighteen years were changing massively. I was finding the letting go of my son to adulthood a challenge but almost always had the gnawing reminder that he was leaving home in September. Whilst I knew logically, that I have done a great job as an encouraging, supportive and positive mum, I was also a very sad one. Sad for me, at losing the life that I have loved with Joe. The logical part of my mind was telling me to focus on the new start and the joy that would bring, but in that moment, it didn't feel like it was possible.

Coupled with letting my hard worked business go, it felt like two babies were leaving me and it felt too much. Looking back, I was so incredibly emotional and really not sure which path to take. One moment I felt certain, the next I had doubts.

The only certain thing was that I was exhausted on every level. Before I began my first business I was very tired. I put a lot into everything that I do, I am very conscientious and proud of that, but single *"mumdom"* as I call it, business owner and mental illness added in, and it's no surprise really.

My purpose in life now felt very confused. Mum and business owner were beginning to feel like redundant roles.

I always knew that I wanted to help people who have experienced similar to what I have. When what felt like every moment was a big, big struggle, a large reason for writing my books has always been to share my personal story of what helped me. I was feeling that maybe I could just keep writing forever and ever. Turn my writing into books, sell my books, help people and live my life like that. Even then in my discontent and emotional state of being, it felt very appealing; writing comes so naturally and I so love to put pen to paper. I was thinking that my rambles about even mulling over all of this may help someone else reading it, and now, here it is in book number 2! I know that kind of book of shared experience and coping mechanisms has helped me before.

To have so many thoughts continually is the norm for me, although I do effectively meditate, they soon return and it can be exhausting. Add onto that feelings from others and myself, as an HSP (highly sensitive person) and it's a roller-coaster ride.

During that time of discontentment, I was having three thoughts for my future self:

One, I create a business around my book, speaking, mentoring and courses. Two, I get a job and become employed again. I didn't think I would ever actually say this, but I was desiring to help people and there were many interesting roles that I could apply this to, be great at and get regular income. Three, I take a complete break and not work at all for a while until I get my energy and focus back. This last choice sounded very desirable.

I had a lot to consider and decide on. Trying to attempt this, in a sleep - deprived state was not the best idea. I knew I was in a big transition in many ways. Being in the moment always remained a challenge for me – my inner motivation and lack of patience wanted results, and fast!

The only way I saw forward, was letting go of working very, very hard and it being anxiety fuelled, to trusting in the universe to provide me with what I need after I had set my intentions. I had proof that this worked, but I was forever slipping in and out of the two opposing states. No wonder my head was cabbaged.

4

My Thing

After another turbulent week and feeling that more of my inner world had been tipped upside down, I came to the conclusion that I had not I been quite prepared for the level of mind chaos writing my book so fast would deliver. That was me all over though – all or nothing. Every day I had new thoughts about old thoughts, bringing me new conflict and feelings to deal with. I decided to make no firm decisions about anything important for the time being and just to allow the turmoil to settle, like a stormy ocean to a calm one. My friend Jane, who is a lovely counsellor, said that it was just my feelings processing and to give myself time. I guess I was panicking myself as I felt all of the feelings at once.

I awoke from yet another vivid dream about people from my past. Immediately it hit me, my Joe, my love was leaving in just six months time. I sobbed into my pillow and I tried to rationalise it again in my mind; but the searing heart wrenching emotions took over. I grabbed my phone and googled *"empty nest syndrome"* searching for some comfort. I read what I already knew between my sobs. This, however, was more, this was something on a deeper level, it always had been for me, the story of my life.

No matter what I do in life and the experiences I have, I feel everything so completely and utterly deeply, it can be intolerable. When it's something exciting and happy, it feels over the top amazing! But when it is something not so positive I feel like I drown in the feelings, it's so incredibly painful.

The logical reassuring side to me looked analytically

at what was going on right now. Joe leaving home was a trigger, it was both a sad and happy time. Whilst so proud of him and excited for his future as a young man and all the joys it can bring, I was bereft with my own grief at letting go. I got this, I understood this, but what I didn't understand, was the depth of my feelings. I felt that I ought to understand possibly by now, I'd been this way for forty six years, I don't know any other way. It's what I've always lived with and at certain times the pain is overwhelming and I frantically search for a way out as I cannot bear it; my heart literally feels like it's going to break, shatter into pieces. Managing and regulating my emotions has been a life long struggle.

I have for a long time, identified myself as a highly sensitive person. I read Elaine Aron's book many years ago and joined a meet-up group for sensitives, and it was a wake up call for me as I related deeply to her descriptions. There is something about loss; the sadness goes way beyond what it should do. It cuts me in half when nothing really bad has actually happened, a 'storm in a teacup' so to speak. Years ago, during intense counselling, my counsellor identified the significance of the struggle I had with endings, right down to how I couldn't wait to get rid of toothpaste when it was coming to an end. As ridiculous as it sounds, it's true.

I can only think this is something to do with when I was a baby or a young child as other therapists have also spotted my intense struggle with letting go. There is some element about being left alone in the world and feeling that agony of abandonment but it's more than that. I have worked so hard on those feelings and have overcome a lot of that struggle. I cannot seem to identify exactly what else it is, as it has never gone away. Any triggering event and it jumps right back out and smacks me in the face and in my heart with a force like nothing else I have experienced. It leaves me feeling unable to function normally - it is all consuming. It has to be something trapped in my subconscious that has never been uncovered. After all, how can you change something when you don't know what it is? You can work on your coping strategies, which I have intensively for years and years. I want to know what my *"thing"* is, to unearth it, explore it and let it go to free me from the suffering it creates for me.

I got up from my bed and wiped away my tears and ate breakfast, then got ready for the day. I said goodbye to Joe, attempting to show little emotion in case it set me off again. On the journey into town, I was fighting back the tears. On my walk to the train station, I came across several homeless people. I felt for them and stopped to talk to one lady and I gave her some change, then I asked about her story. Only twenty nine, with two children in care, she had fallen prey to drugs in order to cope with her pain. Now homeless for six months and dishevelled, bless her. I offered comfort and encouragement at the same time fearing it could be me in her place. This is how out of control my feelings felt right then. I stopped to buy some fruit and bought extra to give to a homeless man outside of the shop. At the train station, my mum called and I started to get tearful again as I explained that I didn't know what was happening to me. She made me feel loved and cared for.

5

The Invisible Girl

With just six days to go until my book was launched I'd been stressed out for the last couple of weeks on working on such a tight deadline for something that meant so much to me. I felt so pressured but most of all by myself, but I could not lose the book launch opportunity. It all came good in the end, and I heaved a great big sigh of relief as I sent all of the artwork and ISBN number off to the printers to let them work their magic. The anticipation of seeing my book in the flesh was building and it started to feel a lot more real. As up until then, I had felt a mixture of excitement, apprehension, worry and not at all believing it was actually my reality. With this relief, came a shift in my mood. The darkness that comes with intense worry lifted and I felt more like *"me"* again after weeks of not. I guess my stirred up emotions were settling down again.

That same day, I also had the privilege to listen to and mentor a young teenage lad. Hearing his troubles and being able to offer him coping strategies and food for thought felt fantastic, especially when I received a text message to thank me. That in itself, made all of my pain feel worth it. If I could use my suffering to help alleviate others with theirs, then what a blessing is that? The old saying, *"A blessing in disguise"*.

I think back to me as a teenager and the painful struggle it was just to exist. I've read that you can remain trapped in the most traumatic time of your life if you do not heal. Until just a few years ago, I could cry when I was around happy teenagers. If only I'd have known that today, fast forward thirty years, I would be helping people like me; that would have really helped me move forwards and heal when I needed it most. Of course, there would be no way of knowing that, but for anyone reading this, it may be a thought to consider. It may bring you some comfort, to think that you may be feeling really awful right now but one day you may be helping someone like you. I find that so comforting for you, because when we can find goodness in bad, the light in our darkness, we have achieved something incredible.

With the shift in mood and the wonderful mentoring session, I truly realised how fulfilling it was to be making a true difference in someone's life as it had been what I was wrestling with for the past two years. Knowing what I wanted to do, but not sure of my path to get there, I am so grateful to that young person for helping me gain some clarity in the chaos.

I spent the next few days before the book launch resting and preparing myself. I wanted to choose the words I wished to speak and clear my mind, whilst remaining connected to my purpose. I also took the time to congratulate myself as I hadn't always been kind to myself in the month prior to completion; I had allowed worry to take over somewhat. I realised I was proud, super proud, of my book and for all it stands for – the young person I was, the *"invisible girl"* and all she went through and coped with bless that girl.

6

The Launch

The night before my book launch I went to the cinema with my close friend Jen. It helped my anxiety as I was starting to ask myself *"Shit, what have I done?"* The thought that in a few hours time I would be revealing my innermost thoughts and *'secrets'* was hugely daunting now it was so close and becoming real. Real, as real as it gets; my words, in print, not just spoken, and also on Amazon. Wow.

The day came round and I was all a-glow. The tweeting was frequent, as it had been in the run up to launching, and connecting with all kinds of wonderful people that were coming to me. I was a bit sad that Joe could not join me but he had college to attend and exams were looming, then had his tutoring job straight afterwards on a Wednesday. I chose to wear a new dress, bought for the occasion. I wore my favourite colours, teal and blue. A cobalt blue shift dress teamed with a teal wrap-over and teal accessories.

My parents were so supportive, from driving me and my boxes of books and point of sale to and from the venue, to my mum staying the whole event and standing with me on my stall. Seeing my stand set up for the first time was emotional, as I carefully laid my pride and joy, my first book, out on the table and stands that my dad had cleverly designed and created. The point of sale looked fabulous and I felt very proud of everything in those hours that followed. Friends came to support me and hear my talk too which meant a lot to me that day, as I was opening my inner most secrets up to the world. It was quite remarkable to meet with and speak to people all day long and hear their stories and answer questions of people that were struggling. That touched me more than I could have prepared myself for and even though I'd seen myself book signing for years in my mind's eye, actually doing it for real was something entirely different. People told me that my happiness glowed outwardly and sure enough, feeling self-respect and pride in myself and my author abilities was new to me and I bloody loved it!

There were some tears from my mum, I think speaking on her behalf they were a mixture of happiness for her daughter and of some sadness as we were recalling the past. However that was the past and a long time ago at that, I was only a child then for the main part of it. Someone mentioned to my mum that she must have found it hard that day – which made me wince and a feeling of guilt started to creep in but I swiftly reminded myself of my reasons. Guilt, which is always a wasted emotion, had drowned me for years as it was, regrets over all kinds of incidents and my behaviours. Blimey, to think I'd punished myself perpetually for years, but now I refused to deliberately do that. It was all what it was, with those doing the best they thought at the time, including me. There is freedom in that for all concerned, forgiveness and releasing resentments was key to peace and joy, and to have the ability to focus on the now and look forward to a happy future.

My instant emotional thought reaction that found its way into my head in that moment, came in quite the explosive manner: *"Sam, they must think what a cruel person you are to be putting your own mum through this"*. That was the Sam's way of thinking from the past, always finding a way to add salt onto an open wound just to hurt myself that bit more. Sam's second thought immediately turned to *"No Sam, you did this with a good intention, not to hurt anyone but to reach out and help actually, and I'm proud of you for your compassion. My mum knows the truth and if anyone is to think that of me, they can and it's none of my business".*

7

The Book Tour

Adjusting to becoming an author was an exciting dream come true for me! As far back as I can remember it had been a main dream of mine. I visualised myself all grown up, writing to my heart's content and holding my very own book in my hand. I'd see myself signing my book for my readers, and speaking on a big stage to hundreds of people. You'd never believe that I was the shyest, most timid little girl who never said boo to a goose, my dream was so far removed from who I was, however I did love to write and was continually encouraged by my school teachers. I loved the opportunity to express my feelings through words, especially when vocalising them felt too hard. Not only would it feel difficult, but I'd feel unworthy of the words I wanted to say. Writing them down made it feel a little less daunting and revealing somehow; God, that girl had been so self-conscious.

Each day I'd wake up with a big grin attached to my face and I'd ask myself *"Am I really an author?"* Followed by a quick *"Yes!"* Shouted out in glee. I actually jumped around in excitement in my lounge at the mere thought, my son Joe, already knew what I was like and it gave him another opportunity to gently poke fun at me. I loved being an excited, passionate and enthusiastic person – they were my strengths and yes I was prone to extremes.

As the Amazon book reviews flooded in, I knew exactly why my soul had told me to write my book. It was releasing my firmly held shame, imposed by myself after I'd formed beliefs from what other people had said to me over the years. My imagination could get me into trouble at times as I always thought and felt vividly. I knew that I'd increased their intensity from what I'd added onto it, and used it as further ammunition to hurt myself with; what a horrible pattern of self-abuse. Then, when readers reached out to me personally to say how much my story had resonated with them and helped them, it felt incredible. Totally why I had done it and why it drove me onto sharing my book with the world AND feeling proud and worthy doing so.

I felt empowered to reach out to as many people as possible who would benefit from my story and kind of created myself a regional book tour as opportunities started to open up everywhere for me. Some incredible synchronicities showed up on my path as I aligned to my true self further and further. I met an array of wonderful people on my journey as I attended masses of events – well-being themes, book fairs and mental health gatherings. I met a lady by *"chance"* at an event who had also been to Chester Lodge, which for a small unit that can only house a few people at a time was astonishing. We felt an instant connection and a knowing of what we each would have experienced. She bought my book, which meant a lot and she knew it would be an emotional read for her. We connected on Facebook also and arranged to meet for a coffee. It was comforting to meet up and share our own experiences of being in a teenage psychiatric unit, and receiving far from *"normal"* teenage years. I believe we were each put on one another's paths for that reason.

As the weeks went by, my own further realisations flooded in. There was never anything wrong with me as a young girl, I was simply reacting to my environment yet I had always sought a label to make sense of myself as if I was someone broken that needed fixing because I felt so different. I had so many awful memories that haunted me, it sometimes warped my perception of others. When I expected a certain behaviour/reaction, then I often got it, this reaffirmed my belief and it increased. I knew that society dictates that we need help and labels us – therefore we believe we have a problem. This is exactly what had happened to me, I'd become a product of mental health labels, partly self-induced. If I had a label I'd also be likely to be taken more seriously which I never felt I was as a young person, and often not as I grew older.

Feelings of invalidation were the most painful and where my feelings of being invisible started. Invalidation ran deeply through my veins, as though I could have been screaming at the top of my lungs and my voice would have fallen onto deaf ears. However, if you put a medical label to it, then I had to be listened to, because there were symptoms, there was evidence that couldn't be missed. What I believed, I became, and it had ended up as a self-fulfilling prophecy. It became clearer and clearer as the pattern of my life emerged with such precise clarity that it was impossible to miss. I was finding many new trains of thought emerge as I read more and listened within, including: If nothing exists, is everything simply a perception we have thought up? For example; Someone seems angry. If I say to myself *"I'm sorry, I love you,"* my thoughts of their anger will subside, then they appear different to me. I'd carried hate and anger within me for years, mostly at myself but also feeling that others had hated me and by turning it to love, my world was changing.

I regularly had interest from therapists, and received opportunities to speak at places I would not normally have been invited to without my book, and for that I was truly grateful. As every time I spoke about my journey, it would release a little more shame and step me into feeling more empowered. My book had helped me to shift a lot of my shame, and knowing I had reached others to resonate with me was powerful as I had a huge desire to turn my pain into a purpose. If I couldn't, what was the point? My past was all starting to make great sense as I became more and more aware of what had happened to me as a younger person and that I had carried all my insecurities, somewhat heavily and clumsily into adulthood. It was only now, with my awareness, that it was time to put the weighted baggage down; I was done with that shit. It may be gradual but I was not prepared to hold onto it anymore, the real Sam was emerging.

8

A New Diagnosis?

Several months after my book was launched: During all of the incredible opportunities and people I met, as well as the synchronicities that never ceased; the recollections of my past and my new understandings of them took a much clearer shape. I realised how many painful memories I had locked within for so many years and how I had pushed them down repeatedly. I'd released a lot of them now and although painful my soul knew it was for my greater good, my long awaited advanced healing.

I do believe that for many years the label (yes I don't like them but this fit like a glove and yes I am referring back to those bloody labels but this is a little different as seen below) Borderline Personality Disorder (BPD) would have explained one hell of a lot. The books I'd read after writing mine and the shock of how much therapy I'd had without much relief, made sense with this label. My GP said he'd thought it very likely with what had happened in my life but wouldn't diagnose me when I requested help. The appointment for a group assessment had now come through and I felt in two minds about going. Part of me felt I was being drawn back into a past I wanted to forget and I had a realisation about this; I had instinctively reacted in panic as I had always done, thinking there was something fundamentally wrong with me and it must be sorted out quickly - my default setting. I'd considered myself to be so many labels and god knows what else over the years in a frantic search to help myself as my feelings were of such unbearable intensity to cope with.

The founder of DBT, dialectic behaviour therapy (recommended treatment for BPD) claimed that some people were wired differently and experienced intense emotions on a scale greater than many. I agreed, as it was the intensity of mine that had created me my problems in the past and even now, look at what was still happening. Knowing this was a little soothing however. Another realisation was that even though a psychiatric ward is a horrible place to be, it also brought me a strange sense of comfort as it always had when I thought about it. There was a safety attached, even though it never felt it once there. I started to fantasise about going into a ward, something I had not done for years, since my mid-twenties. I think that as I went into Chester Lodge, the teenage unit when I was so young and was there for the 16 month duration, it had institutionalised me without my realising and that became my default when I got into a major panic and meltdown, it felt the solution.

BPD is a vile name and it very much makes the person feel ashamed, I did saying it and admitting it to myself if that had been my struggle all along. It is highly taboo, considered very hard to treat and not widely talked about as the name itself insinuates there's something wrong with the person themselves at their core, whereby all it means is a collection of painful traits that have been learned in order to cope with trauma and shut it down - I knew all about that. The problem being, that the traits themselves are very troublesome and make living a free life impossible. Looking back to my twenties and into my thirties, this would have explained a lot of my behaviours as it raged under the surface. I could be highly erratic because of how deeply I felt something, how impulsive I could be, the fear of being alone and rejected and splitting, now that was a really tricky one to contend with. One moment you have feelings of adoration for someone, then they only have to do a little something you don't like and you can feel hate for them in an instant. You also know that is irrational but feel powerless to stop it. There were other issues but these had remained a constant over the years.

Anyhow, I decided to go to the appointment, as my curiosity got the better of me. On the bus journey there I felt teary, as it was bringing back horrible memories of being in a really bad place in my life. As soon as I walked into the hospital building the feelings of gloom hit me; I wanted to run. I stayed and a few minutes later a group of us *"patients"* were gathered in a room and sat in a circle with two therapists. I felt very out of place, uncomfortable and knew I didn't need to be there, I had made a mistake. I couldn't stand the negativity in the room, even the two therapists seemed very negative, it was awful. People around me were clearly very upset and in need of help. I don't mean to sound judgemental in any way, as I really am not but I knew that I did not belong. Years ago yes, I'd have fitted right in but how helpful that actual environment would have been, I am not convinced, but not now. I'd moved forwards in leaps and bounds, despite my recent turmoil, I had got to the place where I had lived a reasonably secure life for years. Holding down jobs for lengthy periods, always supporting myself financially and emotionally, starting a business and being a great mum. That may not sound a lot to some but for me and my past, it was a huge achievement.

I felt greatly for the other people in that room and empathised but it brought me down to be there. I mentioned this to one of the therapists in the break and I must have pressed his buttons as he gave me a condescending retort which really angered me. I'd been polite but explained that I did not feel I needed to be there and explained about my release of emotions surrounding my book etc. It reminded me of how I'd been patronised before by mental health professionals, disgusting. These days I took no shit and challenged him rather than accepting it as my truth.

After filling out a very detailed form in the second half of the session, after people had cried and blew up in desperation after it was revealed they had to go back on a waiting list (I knew that pain so well) I left and as I walked away I vowed I was never going near one of those places again. I felt desperate - to return to my normal life!

It was such an important lesson for me though which I was grateful to learn. If I had listened to what I'd been told, I would have gone down that route, believing I was sick, needed more therapy and needed to be fixed. My flaws - if you want to call them that - were of feeling deeply, but that in itself can also be put to positive use, which I had learnt to do these days. Sure I had times of turmoil, but show me a human that doesn't! Fuck, another realisation – I'd always accepted and searched for my labels which had hindered the problems and one of the reasons why I never moved forwards, needing to fit into a box. The beliefs had been so strong; understandable as professionals, and myself had labelled me since the age of 15. What was actually wrong was what was going on around me, coupled with my highly sensitive self so all of the pain was magnified. Christ, what a journey and it was why I felt I'd lost a lot of my life and why I now chose to live life to the max as much as I could.

8

A New Purpose?

After the pressure I'd put on myself throughout my first business, this time I was operating differently. My book and its realisations was the turning point for living my true life, honouring myself, and being. I read a lot more about the law of attraction and manifestation, and I came to the conclusion that my imagination was so vivid, but had been put to unhelpful use a lot in the past, so I may as well re-frame it all and create myself my dream life. I deserved it and finally felt that to be true.

So returning to the considerations that I'd pondered over a few months ago, I did want to continue working for myself, I really did not want a boss or to lose the freedom I had. I'd always been trying to fit myself as a square peg into a round hole with employment, and yet, the happiest times were when I'd been field based – more freedom! I was most definitely a free spirit and wanted the space to use my creativity and live a life on my terms, now that I had a much firmer sense of who Sam was, free of ugly labels and self-inflicted ones.

As I allowed my mind to take me to the places visually of where I longed to be I was stepping more onto an aligned path. This is ridiculously hard to do when you don't know who you really are or are confused; impossible actually. The more aligned I was becoming, the more I was attracting opportunities to me as my soul was no longer prepared to hustle. Ugh! It filled me with horror to think about forcing myself as I'd spent a lot of my life doing, often in an attempt to feel accepted and liked by others – at a cost to myself. What happened naturally was that people I didn't know previously, mostly, reached out to me for help to write their stories.

Something that I'd never considered was ghost-writing. An opportunity to potentially do this came up and I grabbed it feeling sure that I could not only do it but be great at it! The client initially turned me down as he'd just signed another writer up after we'd had a discussion, so I continued with my author book tour. I had also created an online programme to help people who had experienced emotional neglect and living with the aftermath, so these two areas were my focus. I had a few clients, but knew it wasn't my path of truth so left that to pursue the writing world.

As my life was now being allowed to happen, a few months later, this client came back to me, I believe that I manifested it. The day before I'd been to see a beautiful film with my mum and I said afterwards "if that had been me in that experience I'd have had to write about it" and got excited imagining that. The next day, I received an email asking me if I was interested in still being a ghost-writer for this person's book. Of course I leapt at the chance! He had an incredible story and I wanted to do justice for him and recognised he needed to heal because he had never shared it with anyone before except his wife and the previous writer. So, we met and the story telling began using the notes the journalist had created and a series of recorded interviews. I loved this – it was perfect and as I'd always had a keen interest in journalism in my youth this was similar to my original thoughts, but more suited to me.

I formed a collaboration with the person who helped me with my book creation to offer a complete book writing and design service and a newly branded company was emerging in the early planning stages. Lots of exciting ideas and aims were on the horizon – the possibilities felt endless. My god, releasing my story into the public domain was the best thing I had ever done, for my own healing, to inspire others and now look, it had birthed a new purpose entirely. It was all meant to be!

Some people who were enquiring about help to write their books, wanted to do it themselves with my guidance as my book sales were going from strength to strength. It was enthralling to think that little old me had done this. I sat down and put together a book mentoring programme, a clear step by step guide to how I'd approached my book and added in extras that I'd picked up since. I knew that I was onto something, people really wanted this and it amazed me how many people could relate to my story and how they felt inspired to share also. How beautiful and I gave thanks to the ripples this would create for the world helping so many.

10

University Abound

I think the excitement of my new purpose unfolding was actually perfect timing as it distracted me from my sadness of the thought of Joe leaving home to begin his new life at the University of Nottingham. I'd certainly been going through pre-emptive grieving for some time, at least a year in advance. Again, I put the abnormal label on myself over this, as I'd never heard of it before. Mum's crying yes, but not until their kids had left home. The self-critic within not wanting to miss an opportunity to bite! Each visit to the individual universities on their open days had been mixed with excitement for Joe and his blossoming future and tinged with my feeling of anticipatory grief. I think I was preparing myself but at the last university open day we went to, when the time was drawing closer, the feelings of sadness overwhelmed me and I could not help the tears falling as we were all situated in the main hall for an introduction talk. I had to force down what could easily have been an almighty sobbing session; it felt too real.

Intertwined with my grief of Joe leaving was the powerful reminder of how much love I had for this wonderful person coming into my world, and for giving me a reason to want to heal, to learn to like and eventually love myself. He gave me a feeling of worth that I had not really felt before and in my mix of emotions I was scared of losing that worth I believe. Logically I knew it wouldn't happen as I was a completely different person to almost twenty years ago, but how the mind can trick you. The attachment felt intense and I had to work a lot on focussing on my now and my bright future.

My heart went out to every mother and father going through this stage of their parenthood, the letting go of your child to branch out on their own was harder than I'd ever imagined it would be. They say that nothing prepares you for having your first baby and it doesn't, but nothing prepares you for this either. My mum had said that she'd felt such a loss when I left home, and I remember thinking what an exaggeration, but it wasn't, I was in bits.

There were the worrying motherly concerns – would he be okay in his new accommodation? Would he make good friends? Would he cope with being away from home? Would he manage the workload? Would he meet a girl? Would he… would he? I could have driven myself insane with questions. I felt a reasonable amount of confidence that I had prepared him well to fend for himself and he was a smart lad anyway. It was me that needed looking after right now!

In the few days running up to D Day, his leaving date, I was beside myself and tried hard not to let Joe see me so upset, I desperately didn't want him to worry about me. I knew I'd be okay, it was this leaving bit, it was excruciating. The lounge fast resembled a warehouse with piles of boxes, crates and bags stacked up everywhere. We only just had room to sit on the corner sofa, it was actually amusing to compare the lounge and then Joe's barren bedroom, stripped of almost all of his belongings. It increased the sad feelings when I went into his sparse room, like he'd gone already.

I made the most of my time with him that week, relishing every moment, these times were so precious. Our children grow up so fast, and the one thing we can never retrieve is time and I was so grateful of the happiness Joe had brought into my life. In my mind, I flashed through his 18 years, from the days of baby talc smells and nappy changes, to the lively toddler days to the antics of becoming a schoolboy. Then we had the teen years, where I'd seen major changes in him as he really left childhood behind and he became more of a friend as we enjoyed days out, holidays and he was a great little companion; a love that is so unconditional and like no other love there is. Being a single mum for such a long time, since he was three, had strengthened our bond, we had spent so much time in one another's company, it was like a part of my heart was being ripped out.

The day arrived and I woke up very early. For some reason I felt compelled to get up and do a big pile of ironing while watching a film, it was my way of coping I suppose. When Joe woke up, I made him breakfast and tried to comprehend that he was going away in just a couple of hours time. His dad turned up and we loaded everything into the car, there really was only just enough space for me to squeeze in the back as Joe sat in the front with his dad. I had to fight the tears all of the way. God it was painful. I tried to behave differently and keep an upbeat appearance for Joe's sake, I just longed for the leaving part to be over.

It was busy at the university with cars overflowing the car park and people milling around everywhere. It was a beautiful spot, very green and the campus was like a mini world all of its own. It took several journeys from the car boot to Joe's room unloading all of his worldly goods. His room was small and it felt like one of many in a rabbit warren. As we helped him to unpack it felt surreal, I felt for him and all of the newness he was to experience. Neither I, nor his dad, had been to university, he was breaking new family ground and I was already very proud of him. We said hello to a few faces we came across in passing in the corridor and once most boxes and bags had been emptied into his new space we wandered over to one of the many cafés for lunch together. This felt a little odd anyway as we hadn't been the traditional nuclear family for many years and it was few and far between that we sat together to dine. It was fine though, many other families were doing the same as we glanced around. Hmm I wonder if Joe will be friends with them, or maybe them?

After lunch we drove to a nearby big supermarket to get in many essentials to ensure Joe was well stocked. A trolley full of groceries and other home comforts later (his student staple vodka to share with new friends was already purchased and stashed safely on his bookshelf) we were back at this strange new place he'd now be calling home. His bed was made, I wanted to do the last little things I could for him. Waves of intense grief washed over me back in his little room, I could feel my face trembling and suddenly I announced we should leave, after we'd taken a few photos and had given him the biggest of hugs. I couldn't help but cry, I could not physically push the waterworks down a second longer. It was the first time Joe looked a bit emotional, and I made a hasty retreat to the car followed by Michael, his dad.

I knew Joe would be okay, he'd wanted to go to university for as long as I could remember as he'd always thrived at learning, especially when it came to maths. I knew I'd be okay, once I'd had a damn good cry. I sobbed my heart out all the way back home in the car picturing him standing in that new room on his own, Michael was kind and supported me. Very close to home, one of the tyres blew, and I stood on the roadside feeling like a lost panda eyed soul while the tyre was swapped over.

The next few days I felt very sad and the house was so very quiet. Each time I went into his room I cried at its emptiness. We kept in touch and I looked forward to our contact via Facebook video calls mostly or chats on the phone. He seemed to settle in quickly which really helped, if he was okay, I was okay. And do you know what – I was okay. Within the space of about a week, I really settled down and the sadness really lifted. I was surprised but this anticipatory grief obviously had been what I'd experienced, a lot of the feelings of loss had been felt in advance. I embraced my new version of life and I soon got used to cooking for only one. Batch cooking was a saviour as it was true what they said about cooking for one – it felt bothersome most of the time. I didn't want to slip into unhealthy habits of eating junk foods and it was a godsend to take out a home cooked meal from the freezer at the end of a busy day.

I threw myself into my new purposeful business and spent a great deal of time with my head in my laptop, writing furiously, determined to complete my second book, albeit for someone else this time.

I went to see Joe not that long after him leaving, with my mum, as it was my birthday around that time, I was so excited to see him! We spent a lovely day altogether, he proudly showed his grandma and me around the university, before we went into the city centre for a delicious lunch at a rather quirky café we found. Catching up on his news, it was reassuring to see his relaxed self and happy face. It was a little sad to say goodbye at the end of the day, but he knew that me and my mum could be soppy at the best of times. Big hearts do that to you.

11

An Award and a Night At St Pancras Station

After a rather frantic morning of a meeting, telephone calls, planning for a new book, emails and last minute travel arrangements, I squeezed myself into my ruched red dress and gathered together my travel essentials – namely my phone, train tickets, make up, deodorant, perfume, money, ipod and brand new business cards.

Sitting at the train station in Leicester, with time to kill and a large steaming hot latte, it struck me as rather amusing to be sitting there at two thirty in the afternoon, dressed up like a dog's dinner. I inwardly chuckled.

The journey to London was fast, in just under an hour - I listened to music all of the way, feeling a tad apprehensive now but with a sense of excitement building. At the other end, I topped up my oyster card and two short tube journeys later and I found myself at Canada Water tube station.

Leaving the underground heat behind, I stepped out into the cold dark early evening. I had no idea of where I was, only that the hotel was not far away. Relying solely on my Google maps phone app, I started to walk, twenty minutes it claimed. The route soon took me onto dark and relatively deserted paths, not my idea of fun, I never did like the dark.

Before long, the directions led me into wooded area, I had no choice but to continue the path. I started to feel really afraid, as I was totally alone traipsing in pitch-dark woods, the app insisting I was heading the right way. Every now and then I heard shuffling in the bushes and spotted foxes darting about. I hurried along, cursing every step of the way, promising myself that this would make a great chapter of my book as I went. My feet started to hurt, rubbing on my evening shoes and I was concerned that I'd arrive at the venue muddied up, looking like I'd been on some forest trek rather than ready for an evening of awards. I tried to see the funny side and compared it to a scene out of *"The Blair Witch project"* whilst feeling fearful.

I came across about three people on this route, which seemed to last forever and just about jumped out of my skin. I took a few wrong turnings, even with the Google guidance, my sense of direction was never my strongest point. I began to think I was never going to find it as it took me about twice the recommended time and seemed the most unlikely route. I'm sure in the daytime it would be lovely, as I was around Docklands, but at night it was scary. Very suddenly, I came out of the woodlands and onto a main road and there was the illuminated sign for the hotel. I breathed such a sigh of relief, I was here and still alive!

I wasn't convinced at first that it was the right hotel, as the location seemed so odd, but thankfully the reception confirmed it was. With an hour to go, I decided on a drink in the bar. With London prices so steep I settled for a cider and sat down to charge my phone up. A few minutes later, an older lady entered the bar and looked a little lost. I ushered her over and invited her to sit with me after realising she was here for the Awards evening too. I warmed to her straight away and not long into our conversation, she told me she was here to speak tonight. This followed onto what she did, and this lady only turned out to be Irma Kurtz, the agony aunt for Cosmopolitan magazine for over forty years - I was blown away! I used to love her column in my twenties and thirties. I actually felt rather star struck but she was so lovely and down to earth. I listened with interest as she told me about her writing career.

We were gradually joined by some other guests, some people that had travelled from the USA especially for tonight, other authors. It was incredible and I was so excited for the evening ahead. We all transferred from the bar to our function room for the evening. I delighted in a champagne reception and the chance to be photographed and interviewed about my nominated category, Author Of The Year. Mingling with some of the other guests, everyone in their glamorous outfits, a special atmosphere was growing. I met another lady that has been incredibly inspiring in her work, also one of the speakers. I had already met her daughter a couple of times so struck up a conversation, she was charming and a self-confessed Dame Judi Dench lookalike!

Going through to the main function room which looked stunning, I was seated between Irma and Deborah. I was still chuckling inwardly to myself. Evi, who had nominated me in the first instance had been delayed, as I sporadically checked my phone for updates. She'd had a last minute change of plan for her journey and was arriving with two other people, including another nominee. I had never even met Evi before, but we had shared many online conversations and felt as though we knew each other a little. Well actually she felt that she knew me rather well, and I reminded her that she had read my book of my life story, warts and all!

The evening began with a brief welcome from our beautiful hostess Placida, the brains behind the event itself and then we kicked off with some entertainment. I was, unwillingly at first, coaxed onto the dance floor with most of the room, to salsa. It turned out to be good fun as we all tried in vain to keep up with the fast yet graceful moves from the teacher. After what seemed the equivalent to a mini gym workout, we all got to sit back down. Then we heard from an interesting speaker talking all about Sickle Cell, whilst we dined on the succulent Caribbean feast. Sumptuous jerk chicken, curried goat and fish fritters, all divine.

Suddenly I felt someone grab me and give me the biggest squeeze…it was Evi - bless her. How lovely to meet her after our intense conversations online. She was so sweet and very petite. I moved my table so that I could sit with her and the two other ladies as we had booked to do. The wine flowed and the speakers shared the stage. All the time I had three inner thoughts, was Joe okay at home with his mates coming round, was I going to get my last train home okay as the evening was a little behind schedule and the tension building for the award announcements.

Irma's talk was entertaining and endeared me further towards her - such a special lady. Deborah's talk was very inspiring as was the final speaker. We were entertained with more dancing and a vocalist with one of the most powerful voices I've heard, not dissimilar to Tina Turner. We heard again from Placida, herself a sufferer of Sickle Cell, and the compiler of two books written by women. Then these brave ladies were awarded for their triumphs and for sharing their stories. Next, it came to the Awards section towards the end.

By this point, I was a little distracted and was anxious about my train, it was looking unlikely that I would catch it and started to think of what plan B would be. Spending the night at the train station was looking likely, my current budget not stretching to an unexpected London hotel for the night.

The awards were being called out, several categories to go through, wonderful to see the winners being cheered and congratulated. You could tell that everyone in that room was dedicated to their cause, their why, and were driven to achieve what they had. I loved that; Passion and determination, two of my favourite traits in a human. The other nominee I was sat with, thanks to kind Evi also, won her category. I thought that there was definitely no way on earth that I would be chosen too. When they called out my name for the second time, I had to be prompted by my crowd, that they had called my name out, for my category, I had won! I was so shocked and walked over to the stage to collect my award in a daze. I remember grabbing Placida, hugging and thanking her and telling her how much it meant to me. I fought back the tears and then jumped off of the stage in a whoop! I was ushered out of the room for another photo holding my beautiful glass award. It felt so incredibly personal and special to me, as I'd won this for sharing my story. I cannot even begin to explain the depth of that for me, as the former *"Invisible Girl"* and how moved I was by the occasion.

Then it was quite a rush to get our belongings together, call a taxi and try to get me across the city of London in time for my last train. The taxi driver looked harassed as we asked the chances of us making it in time, at this point I resigned myself to the fact that I'd be spending the night in the station. However, nothing could dampen my spirits at this special time.

At around half past midnight, I bid farewell to Evi and her friends. It kind of felt surreal as I realised that I had a long night ahead, with the next train not until a quarter to six in the morning. I made my way to the toilet to freshen up a little. Then I sussed out my ticket and purchased, before finding the few outlets that stayed open all night within St Pancras. I got myself a coffee, I envisioned plenty of those throughout this stretch of time to keep me awake at the very least and settled down in Pret. I was bursting with excitement to tell Joe and my parents my thrilling news. They were over the moon, even though my texts woke my parents up. I sat and pondered over the events of the evening just gone by, how incredible had it been.

People were fallen asleep, with their heads on their bags, sitting at the café tables. I wondered what they were all doing there, as they did not appear to be homeless. As I do, my vivid imagination began to make up little stories about each person and their reason for being stranded at the station halfway through the night. After a while, we were all moved on by the staff, which did make me feel a little like a stray with nowhere to go. Just round the corner was a Starbucks and they stayed open all hours, brilliant. Settling down with another latte, I remained in that seat for about three and a half hours. I begged some paper from a member of staff, rummaged in my handbag for a pen and began to write notes about this evening. I felt this elation within me, I wanted to burst and had to stop myself from standing up and blurting it out to all in the café. I felt so happy and proud of myself; all or nothing Sam!

I donned my headphones and listened to music as I scribbled my notes and mini mind map, designed to prompt memories for writing purposes. I'd always half lived in a fantasy world for when the real one was too hard to be in and it had remained a habit. I found visualisation very powerful for me and it can do so much good. It was as busy in this café throughout the night as it was during the day at a Leicester café, incredible. Quite fascinating to watch the variety of customers there were around me. Late night revellers, including young girls in skimpy clothing, high heels, sandals, fake tanned legs and young lads in short sleeves. It was November for god's sake, smiling as I remembered those rare days in my youth of venturing for a night out totally inappropriately dressed for the season. Then on the other end of the scale, folk bundled up with wintry wear, thick coats, woolly scarves and hats and a blanket or two. I was somewhere in the middle, with my sleeveless dress and faux fur jacket.

There were foreign students, well I guessed they were students, they were young. Travellers with their luggage in tow and a tramp, whom was urged to leave after he received his hot drink. I wondered how many others had missed their trains, maybe the revellers as some were there for the long haul too. A couple were snuggled together covered with a blanket and at one stage moved onto the floor, where they were swiftly asked to move.

Lots of coffees were ordered throughout the time I sat there and late night snacks. The staff kept the shelves and chilled cabinets fully stocked which was strange to see at three o'clock in the morning. I became aware of how chilly I felt at almost four o'clock. Before my train was due, I freshened up again in the toilets, feeling rather scruffy after all of these hours and still in full make up and the same underwear. Not pleasant. I grabbed a takeaway coffee and raisin pastry for the journey and went to board my train. Sitting down, now feeling the exhaustion of the evening's antics but a proud glow and smile plastered across my face, as I was homeward bound.

12

Design Your Life

I remained elated for weeks and was floating on an imaginary bed of air after the awards night. My life was just getting better and better! I attended many events in the run up to Christmas, nowhere near as many as I would have done with Iridescence, my other business mind you! That had been exhausting, every January for four years running, I'd spent recovering after a manic month and half, finally collapsing in a spent heap after the final pre-christmas event. My book was selling really well and each time I felt a swell of accomplishment and gratitude.

I sold off my old jewellery and accessories as a job lot, now only selling a small amount of inspired words silver jewellery alongside my book at events or online. It was a relief to let go of it and create space for new stuff to come through. I was done with that now.

Joe came home for the first Christmas from uni, I felt spoilt having him home again and he knew it! I didn't even mind the dirty washing he had with him. I had adapted to my new lifestyle but it was lovely having him back.

I treated us to a holiday to Lanzarote in the January before he went back and had to study for exams. We both deserved a break in the sunshine after our change of lives and working hard. It was blissful, we loved it there, it was our third visit and good weather in the winter is practically guaranteed. I indulged in my passion for massage almost every day of the holiday! When the ladies came around on the beach I could not resist, why should I? The combination of the warmth, the sound of the waves and the soothing touch of massage is a magical combination not to be missed. We had a super time and came back to a cold old blighty as you'd expect in January.

I've always been the sort to reflect, most likely because of the way my life had panned out, therapy kind of forces you to examine your past to make sense of where you are at. I'd become a master of achieving this and was an incredibly self-aware adult now. Sometimes I feel I can be too aware but it gives me a deep level of empathy for others suffering, and is why I want to write and share and help others to do this too; it's remarkably cathartic. I know that it may have sounded a little traumatic to you reading this after the release of my first book, but remember that book came out of me at a crazy fast rate – 16 days from start to finish. I'd not had time to thoroughly process, but because I had suppressed emotions and memories for such a long time, it was bursting and I couldn't contain the force of it once I'd removed the lid to write. This book has been a different style altogether and has been written in spurts so far, as I focused mostly on my business.

Towards the end of January I came upon the end of the book I was writing for my client. It had been an interesting journey as the story unfolded, it was quite a harrowing experience for this person. As I said, he had never shared most of the intimate details before. I began to recognise the need for quite strict boundaries to protect myself going forwards let's say, it turned out to be a huge learning curve for me.

Not too long after this I encountered some hostility towards me at what I was doing, which threw me off course a little temporarily – I never could understand the need for people to be nasty. If they didn't understand – don't allow ignorance to be an excuse for bad behaviour, there is no need. I'd never had any bad attitude towards me with regards to my book, only people thankful for sharing my story – my Amazon reviews said it all. It never amazed me either how a person or people chose to lash out and then attempt to project it back onto you. It took me some reconnection to my vision and to my heart to shake off this unpleasantness and move forwards again.

Another pattern I saw, was that I'd often been a target for a bully or two. I was a very feeling person who wore her heart on her sleeve, and certain people will attempt to abuse that to make themselves feel better. I put up some defences and boundaries but some personality types were very determined to be destructive to others - sad but true. This is not to say I am perfect, far from it and perfection isn't a real thing anyway. However, I'm not a pathetic pushover either, but I do care about people and always have. I'd had to toughen myself up somewhat in business else I'd have been eaten alive (at times it felt as though I had been chewed a bit!) and often felt that I was too honest for the business world. I'd never really felt that I'd fitted in and admitted to myself that I hated networking as it felt farcical. I was an introvert and a very sensitive one at that and I loved meaningful connections and deep conversations – small talk left me cold. Banter was different; fun and light, and I'd enjoyed this when I did my sales events but it still exhausted me. These experiences made me listen up to what I heard many coaches saying online *"design your life"*. I did just that.

I sat down with a journal notepad and thought deeply about how I wanted my business and lifestyle to be going forwards. There were some non-negotiables and many desires. At the end, I had a clear roadmap of what I wanted and where I was heading. The girl felt on fire again! I wanted to create my entire business online as my long term vision was to travel and feel even freer with few constraints. I craved more balance in my life too and was determined not to revert back to the hustling, just thinking of it was exhausting. No way Jose – this girl had new ways of doing things that truly lit her up.

13

Collaboration

February 2018 brought the official launch of the new business partnership. The launch had a physical launch too and I gained my first mentoring client who had found me on Instagram and came in person to the event. A local lady and she was lovely to work with as we embarked on the book mentoring journey a couple of weeks later. Nicci was my first official book mentoring client, which will always remain a special milestone in my business. She had a very touching story and had always dreamed of sharing it all in a book, bless her heart.

I focused a lot of time and energy on the marketing to build up the new brand, using social media mostly as I always had as it gave me an excuse to write even more (yes I loved this aspect!) and to connect to potential clients this way. I embraced the passion of creating a brand as well, just as I had with my first business, again it gave the opportunity to tell a story – a continual one and I loved this. Once I was clear in my head about goals there really was no stopping me – overall, I ran head first at fears I came up against in my business. Believe me, I had loads as marketing as an introvert can be daunting and took a lot of energy but I did them regardless, and even found myself enjoying Facebook lives and videos. They were one of the best ways to connect to your audience that's for sure, as people got to see the real you and feel your energy. Beliefs were only limiting if you allowed them to be, I wanted to live my most limitless life now I had found my true self. I owed it to her to give myself the best chance of success, of living my best life and of helping others in the process. It had been one hell of a journey to get to this point.

Some more clients found me to help them with their stories and I really fell into my new role with confidence; it felt natural and right.

Joe continued to thrive at uni, and when I thought of how I'd felt only five months previous at the thought of him leaving home, comparing it to how I now felt – it was incredible to witness the growth I'd gone through. I saw it in Joe too and was so happy for him to have settled and made friends.

I had quite a few speaking opportunities still filtering through since my book debut and I always embraced these enthusiastically – any chance to share my message further was a blessing. Although I did not talk so much and promote my book that actively anymore, as the main focus was on building the business, I still continued to get book sales via Amazon and some through social media.

Always a researcher and craving to learn anything that would help me to move forwards in business and in life, I was nearly always on some kind of course, programme or having coaching. This was however a minefield; I could dedicate a whole book to my experiences in that arena, as I could dating, but I'm going to keep it short for the sake of this book. Just a few pointers here, I've had a coach who was costly but decided to go on holiday for a week of her programme and give no learnings stating it as a week of reflection. I was astounded – seeing pics of her beach holiday that I and the other clients had helped to pay for as we were left to our own devices. I'm all for designing a life/business around your own desires but this was taking the Mick!

Then there's been coaches that have wanted to reign my

big thinking in (what!), one that threw me out of her Facebook group after I asked for help, was not given any and spoke up and one that slagged off other coaches! Not pleasant and I'm not sharing any of this to moan, but to let others know they are not alone if they have experienced similar or worse. Business lessons in abundance.

Anyhow, throughout the costly (in time, effort and cold hard cash) coaching experimentation, and I hasten to add, I was always an action taker and coach-able – very coach-able as I want results, I finally came across a superb person that I could totally relate to and felt aligned with. So after some homework, liking everything I saw, I bought one of her books and loved it! See, a book is a perfect low risk way to bring in new clients as you'll see from what I'll go on to share. It complimented my new ways of being and thinking by being in alignment and using the laws of the universe to bring to you what you desire. I completed the book, it was a 21 day workbook and enjoyed the new knowledge and it inspired me to dig deeper into this world of manifestation. I felt a tad disappointed when I didn't get the results that I was after per book, well not straight away at least and that was a lesson in itself.

14

Manifestation

The new business arrangement had a few teething troubles as I expected with anything new. I appeared to have some different perspectives on certain elements of the business to my collaborative partner, which was a bit stressful as we needed to be on the same page to move forward and expand. We kept talking it through which was good and in many ways we were compatible with complimentary skill-sets. Something I believe is important to consider when partnering up – find someone who has different strengths to you.

One major aspect was money and the differing attitudes towards it. For me, as a start-up full of passion I wanted to take a few small risks and do some marketing to get us out there faster as I knew the energy it took to do everything organically from my first business. I had a massive vision, which felt very real to me, and I was motivated to do everything I possibly could to get to that place.

The workbook I'd read recently inspired me to take further action as I felt some minor frustrations in the business. I listened and studied some more of the author of the book and loved everything she had to say. Once the opportunity arose to get into one of her main programmes to learn manifestation, I didn't have to think twice. At this point, so early on in the business, I didn't have the free cash but I was compelled to take action, believing it would propel me forwards so I used one of my credit cards. I was already paying back some of my business debt that had amounted from all of the learning I had undertaken and was paying it back gradually. I believe in investing in myself thankfully, and was open to the right kind of help. Why struggle when help is on hand I say?

I was not disappointed! As soon as I signed up, the energy in the private Facebook group was electric and I was hugely charged up ready to create big changes. The other women in the group seemed lovely too and were of a similar mindset, more on the *"woo woo"* side than traditional entrepreneurs I'd say with a lot of spiritual knowledge and beliefs. It felt like a perfect fit for me since my life had taken me to that path over the past year. The excitement built in the run up to the first session beginning in a few days time, I was already convinced I was going to have big shifts. I just knew it and felt it with all of my might.

Each morning I woke up very excited for the day to start and what it would bring. I hadn't felt this brilliant and motivated since an online business I was involved in briefly a couple of years previously. The mentor of that had been powerful and for 6 weeks I didn't sleep much as I was so wired. This I know is not necessarily healthy or *"normal"* behaviour, and I actually lost weight on a short holiday in that period, which is absolutely unheard of for me! I'd never been the same since in my ability to get as excited, as I was off the scale and when I crashed, boy did I crash. It wasn't long after that I felt my burnout started, before my first book writing frenzy. I wasn't at the same level as that but I felt very happy, light, and super motivated.

I'd got a few clients by this point from my online presence and a speaking opportunity I jumped on at a networking meeting, that was a story all on its on believe me. So for the six week duration of this manifestation programme, I could split my time between these clients, which included writing a new book, marketing the new business and devoting myself to this learning. Intense self-development can really take it out of you energy wise but it's worth it for what it brings to you in return.

The programme begun and it was incredible. I loved the coach's energy and could tell our personal values were similar as I felt incredibly aligned to her, something I have found near impossible to find as a sensitive soul. The buzz from the group was magnificent and I made the beginnings of some new friendships too, mostly with American ladies, of whom I was often drawn to. I love their boldness, confidence and straightforwardness!

I began to see patterns in my money mindset from my past conditioning, as we all do, that I knew were holding me back on some levels, so many business people have this, I recognise it straight away in people now, and I was determined to sort mine out. What is the point in working hard to build a business for you to go and sabotage it? None whatsoever, that's what! It's very common, and when you examine the money stories we are fed from birth it's not surprising many of us have blocks. From your upbringing that focuses on lack, which can be generational – recalling the old sayings such as *"money doesn't grow on trees"* or that *"you have to work hard for money"* and of the continual messages that general society bombards us with from a young age.

The course was fantastic and as I soaked up the new findings and put them into practice I really began to see results in my business and I attracted more and more clients to work with me and other opportunities came in.

15

Exorcising Ghosts

As the business blossomed, and it was purely from sharing the relentless passion about sharing your story as far and wide as possible, I realised more than ever that working on my mindset was crucial to business success. I loved personal development anyway, but now I was really seeing the results I'd worked so hard for the past 6 years. I vowed to always make time to work on my business to grow and improve it, to work on my continued mindset and to work in my business. I yearned to learn more about manifestation and the Law Of Attraction as I felt far more inclined to continue on this path as opposed to the traditional hustle route, which had burnt me out. I also knew it was a journey and frequently flipped between the two states.

I spent less time talking about my own book and focused on helping others to write their stories and get them published, out there doing what they were designed to do. However, I recognised that it was my story that brought the clients and work to me and I truly believed in leading by example. I relished the further opportunities that I met on this new path and three speaking events were great milestones for me.

I was invited to speak at a school to around 140 teenagers and teachers about my story and of following your dream in life no matter what. It was the biggest audience that I'd presented too but I loved it! To speak with teenagers was close to my heart as I knew some of them sitting there in that audience, would be struggling with themselves, possibly silently. If I could help those then how fabulous. One or two came up and spoke to me afterwards, and I know that my younger self was proud of me that day.

Then there was an outdoor well-being festival in the centre of Nottingham – perfect as Joe was already there and I longed for him to hear me speak. My mum joined us too and it was exhilarating to stand on a big stage, in the city centre, with a reasonable sized audience and share from my heart. A lovely sweet lady, Anita, I'd met through reading my book, came to see me speak which was heart warming – we had formed a lovely bond by this point and she was very supportive of what I was doing. I always had people share parts of their stories with me afterwards.

Probably the most rewarding of all, was going in to speak at a medium secure forensic psychiatric unit in Leicester. My heart empathised with these people profoundly as their dark struggles were deep. The deeper the pain the more I empathised. Sadly they were heavily sedated as I imagined they would be but most took a real interest in my talks and we engaged in conversation afterwards. The staff were lovely and that in itself was healing for me, as some of my memories of mental health staff were not fond ones. There was a greatly supportive feel to the place and they especially encouraged lived experience to inspire patients so I was honoured.

They bought several copies of my book for the hospital library which made me so proud every time I visualised my book on a shelf in there. The feedback made me shine brighter still. Before this took place, I deliberately went a little earlier than my appointment time as it happened that the unit was in the vicinity of where Chester Lodge used to be, now pulled down and they'd built a housing estate on the land. On the bus journey travelling there I had tears pricking as I had not gone to that area on foot since my teenage years. All of my memories flooded back and briefly it felt overwhelming, but

I was determined to face my ghosts of the past, my soul was telling me to do this to free myself further.

I felt very sad as I walked through the wooded area next to the houses, some of the adjacent old Victorian asylum ruins still stood and I recalled how I used to look at these every day from the unit. I remember walking down the hill outside the unit to the nearby shop to buy a secret stash of sweets to comfort myself with. Weirdly, I had fantasised about being in this secure unit so that I didn't have to leave a hospital environment, I felt then as though I'd wanted to be locked up and protected from the world forever. After pondering on some of these memories and facing what I had avoided, I reminded myself that that's exactly what they were, memories, not the now. The new me, dried her eyes, composed herself and walked onto the path that lead to the secure unit.

On the subject of exorcising ghosts, there were another two experiences that occurred around this time. I went to an event at my old school, the one where I began to truant from and held a lot of painful memories for me; I was selling my book and it felt significant to do that there. A similar thing happened to me as with the secure unit visit, on the bus journey I went from being okay, happy to welling up with tears. This time I couldn't control them as well and started to sob quietly on the bus, I just couldn't keep them in; I was embarrassed and couldn't wait to reach my stop. I dived straight for the toilets on arrival and got myself together. It was strange being in my old school, full of memories. All I know is that going back to these key locations of my painful past reduced me to a quivering mass of tears. However, once calm, I set up my stall and sold several books and was able to share how some of my story featured that school. I felt a sense of relief afterwards as though a part of me had healed.

From another well-being event that I attended, I met a lady who was a social worker. She took great interest in my story and we connected as she thought that we may be able to work together. She had a friend with her and a few weeks later I went to see this lady as she had reached out to me and said she had been called to speak to me. She happened to live in the area of where I grew up before we moved to the village of Houghton, as I refer to in my first book. I was very surprised this time to find myself teary on the bus journey as it neared my old estate, as this was going back to pre-teen years.

These experiences surprised me, the depth of sadness that I felt on visiting old areas. I had no idea they held that much emotion for me. Maybe I had trapped in so much more than I ever realised?

16

The Summer of 2018

Business grew more and with it being so new, it was evolving a lot. Trying to understand your niche market has to be one of the most frustrating parts to business, but necessary to understand how to reach and who to serve. Some tension began to show in my business collaboration as although we shared some values, some appeared to be quite different and we almost went separate ways as I shared how I felt the relationship felt unbalanced. We worked at very different paces which made it feel unfair, but after a discussion I felt we found a compromise to even the workload out.

Sure I could be wildly impulsive at times, I own that, but I did aspire to get stuff done and was very driven in seeing results and achieving results for our clients. I was madly passionate and felt as though I was at last living on purpose and had a huge vision. One of my impulsive actions was to join a Mastermind group. It was a considerable amount of money from where I was at, at that moment in my new business journey and I'd be responsible for that, but I wanted to embrace all I could to take me further. At these times I often just think *"Sod it"* and take action before stupid fears start to creep in, then it's done and I have to take bigger action. It generally works a treat for me, the sink or swim approach! It excites me and makes me feel alive and I found that it aided my manifestation once I learnt to let go of the attachment to outcome more and just hold that invisible faith and feel the passion.

It proved to be not one of my better decisions and several thousands of pounds later, depleted energy and a feeling of misalignment I left the group. I met some good people but the marketing strategies I was taught did not work for me, as it felt all wrong and not what I believed in. It took me a few weeks to go back to being me.

Summer was upon us before we knew it and Joe passed his first year uni exams. Towards the end of the last term he became a little stressed and I told him to return home and not to be in the environment he didn't need to be in; a mum will always protect. He did, and the summer began. I loved having him back home and the uni holidays were much longer than school or college, I felt spoilt again.

Throughout the summer, which weather wise was a scorcher, I worked a lot on growing the business. I was full of spirit and excitement and kept attracting new clients to work with me. I felt so much gratitude each time a client trusted in me to help them with their story, it was a special honour to do this work. I had my first international clients from Ireland and from the USA. The two ladies, a mother and daughter came to me with a very sensitive story of sexual abuse, from the father. We all connected and over the space of a few months their stories were written. I actually learnt a lot from these two as they were incredibly educated on trauma and the effects. Their stories were courageous beyond belief and every time we spoke and I discovered more of their journey my heart felt for them further. What they went through and to now have the courage to do this, was amazing. I could relate to the trauma bonding, *"Stockholm syndrome"* and of wanting to protect others that have hurt you. By the end of our writing journey together we had forged what felt like a solid friendship too; they were forces to be reckoned with I tell you!

As the sunny and blue sky days persisted, we enjoyed many family barbecues at my brother's house. My mum had read my book, devoured it in one sitting but I think my dad and my brother had only heard about parts of it from my mum. We were certainly closer as a family, guards had been let down, and I felt much closer to them all. Joe read my book too and left me a review on Amazon. He said afterwards how lucky he felt and to be grateful for all he had, that made me cry.

While I was busy Joe wasn't so much. I noticed that after several weeks he seemed to be in what I'd describe as a slump, sleeping in most days, staying up late at night gaming, and not having a great deal of productivity going on in his life. He didn't seem his usual self but insisted he was okay. I did feel concerned but we spoke openly frequently as we always had done. Part of me thought I was worrying over nothing that wasn't normal teenage behaviour, it played on my mind though. I was aware that I should not be concerning myself about things ahead and to focus on the now but it was a major challenge when it came to the health and happiness of my child.

We had two holidays together, one with my family to beautiful Cornwall and one to Turkey just Joe and me. Turkey was searing hot, day and night and was fun. The exchange rate was in our favour so we enjoyed several trips out as well as the relaxing beach and pool days we both loved. I felt lucky that my nineteen year old son still wanted to go away with me and was making the most of every moment as I knew the day would arrive when he wouldn't want to. We relaxed with a traditional Turkish bath – all lovely until they tried to give us a hard sell during the final massage – which kind of ruined the atmosphere somewhat!

The quad biking was fun and fast and we were filthed up

in the dry dusty surroundings even wearing the bandanna's. The boat trip was cool, I love the sea, with stop off's at a stretch of beach with proud looking camels parading up and down the sands. On the return journey, the young lads working on the boat let loose as we had a foam party on board – it was crazy fun! However, the last trip was the most memorable, the Jeep safari. The Turkish guys were crazy on this trip – we couldn't believe it at first as you'd never have gotten away with it in the UK! They drove like madmen through the streets in these bulked up Jeeps, loud music blaring and at least one of them hanging off of each vehicle, jumping off at regular intervals to fire water at us with water guns and plastic bottles. We were given ammunition too and it ended up in one big crazy water fight. We stopped at one place to fill up on water at an outdoor tap which had a stone type of basin underneath it. Before you knew it, the Turks were grabbing unsuspecting guests and dunking them into the basin; then they grabbed Joe! He stood bemused, dripping from head to toe in saturated shorts, t-shirts and watch – yes they didn't stop for those details to be checked. Mayhem! Everyone soon dried off in the heat and the speed that they tore about the land. The lunch stop was stunning, an outdoor restaurant complete with vines and some shelter from the sun. Before the wine was poured and food was served, most of us and the other guests, jumped into the lake we were next to. On the last full day of the holiday Joe banged his nose on the side of the swimming pool, we didn't think any more of it as he was okay. During the holiday, although I relaxed a lot, I had a niggle connected with business but told myself not to think of work while away. Fond memories were made.

The second day we arrived home, I was getting on top of all the usual chores such as washing, washing and more washing, and catching up with business tasks that needed attention. While sitting in front of my laptop, that Sunday afternoon, still relaxed, I received an email into my in box that I couldn't take in at first. It confirmed my niggle that I'd had on holiday as I sensed something was not right but no one had spoken honestly. The email was so nasty it stunned me and it was twisted. After the shock dispersed a little - things like that are really hard to take in as a highly sensitive person as you cannot grasp how someone can be so cruel with their words - I formulated a response. Integrity and truth are really important to me and I needed to speak up about the truth of the matter without the callous words they decided to use so they got themselves off of a hook they no longer wanted to be part of a project that had been embarked upon.

After that I blocked them out of my life as I didn't wish to be around energy such as that, and I realised a few things that my inner sense had been telling me. I refused to be pushed around and manipulated and this particular person wanted me to do exactly as they wanted with no regard to what I felt was right. The contents of the email were very damning and as much as I tried to separate myself, it hurt as they made it very personal while stating that they hadn't. A paradox if ever there was one! They ripped apart my writing skills and claimed they wanted nothing to do with me, knowing full well after such harsh words that would be the last thing I would want, cunning. It helped me to remind myself of all of the wildly successful people we know of that had been put down and dismissed as useless. Walt Disney immediately came to mind.

It took me a while of working on my mindset to build myself up again, but I focussed on the people that did appreciate me. It was hard enough in business anyway to put yourself *"out there"* over and over again. I told myself again and again that it was *"their stuff"* and a reflection of their character, they wanted to pursue others things so why not just be honest? I always seemed to attract bullies, all of my life. Thankfully, I'm not a pushover anymore, I used to be, and will have confrontation if necessary but I just don't like to be aggressive and pushy. Maybe I still needed to have firmer boundaries.

Towards the end of the summer holiday, Joe began to feel a little anxious about returning to uni and going into a shared house. Only a little which I thought was totally understandable. As a sensitive person, I wouldn't give you a thank you to share a house like that. One night he had what transpired to be a panic attack. He had been experiencing a strange feeling in his nose which he was relating to the swimming pool incident and began to believe something was wrong with him. The feelings of physical anxiety built up in him and escalated eventually into panic as he came into the lounge in a state. I was pretty certain it was panic but rang the NHS helpline for reassurance, thinking of the knock in the pool. I helped him to calm down, not having seen him like that before. There was some anxiety when he was little and having swimming lessons but nothing since then. He did calm down but it was hard to convince him that nothing terrible was going to happen to him. I didn't let him see it, but it upset me to see him like that. My first thoughts were that I felt responsible. The mess I had been for years and now look. It was the last thing on earth I'd want for him and I somehow felt to blame as his mum. It seemed an isolated incident but he did keep mentioning this funny sensation in his nose and facial area over the following few days.

Not so long after this incident, and on a weekend where he

spent time with his dad, Joe sent me a message and seemed to be in a panic. I tried to calm him down on the phone and sent him a meditation to do before he came back in a short while. By the time he arrived back, he was not calmer by any means and was experiencing another full blown panic attack. He couldn't sit down as was obviously very agitated and stood at the window gasping for air. He was not my Joe as I knew him. I got him to sit and talked him through some deep breathing and he calmed down quickly as he listened to my firm but soothing words. I remembered when you are in that state, you need someone to be soothing yet firm with you to instil that confidence that you will be okay. Later on he admitted that he'd been mulling over a few concerns mostly about uni and his health, still concerned that something was wrong with him.

Quietly, I pleaded for him to not be going down a path of those struggles. I suggested that he meditate each day, to keep talking when he needed to and to try and eat healthily and exercise. And to ration the amount of time he spent on his phone and social media – this was certainly responsible for creating unnecessary anxiety!

A couple of days later and he was all packed up to return to Nottingham and both his dad and I took him to move into his new house for the year. His house-mates we met seemed lovely and friendly and of course there were the obligatory mum's tears on the journey back. This time though was vastly different to the year before when he first left home. Such a lot had happened in the meantime.

17

Don't Do Things By Halves

When Joe had returned to university I felt able to give my full focus on my business again, when he is home its most important to me to spend time together as we never get that back.

I was lucky to work with some beautiful and sincere people who had incredible stories to share with the world. I threw myself into these and felt most aligned with what I was doing and the great people and opportunities kept on turning up. I felt joyful and excited a lot of the time which confirmed to me I was on the road meant for me. I'd always believed that we were born to feel joy. I got to the place where I seemed able to manifest what I'd been asking for and it excited me greatly!

Over the coming weeks I had phone calls from Joe. We never went that long without seeing one another as I'd often visit him in Nottingham and we'd make a day of it, or he would come home for a long weekend. The feelings of anxiety and worry were becoming troublesome for him and popping up whether he had concerns or not and he was panicked about the sensations especially palpitations. I remembered how horrible that feels and from time to time I had moments. It didn't seem to be improving whatever we tried and spoke about until eventually it was interfering in his daily life considerably and he was on my mind a lot of the time. I wanted to be there for him and we had lengthy phone calls when he needed extra support in between visits. Secretly, I started to really blame myself and felt such guilt as

I cast my mind back to when he was little. As much as I loved him and always wanted to do right by him, I still had my own troubles back then and now I began to believe it was my fault he was suffering. I felt responsible as his mum and asked myself over and over if I had traumatised him as a little boy. It broke my heart as I felt compelled to take that responsibility and make everything right for him again. When he rang me to say he'd not made it into a lecture, or he'd had to leave in a panic, I felt guilty. What had I done to him?

I started to discover just how sensitive Joe was too through our intense conversations and I tried to educate him about being empathic and of energy and how it works. Knowing this would have helped me in my youth but I never heard anyone speak of this back then.

Meanwhile, tensions had mounted with my business partner again and I felt exhausted from trying to make it work. I slipped my business head on, and made a firm decision, I needed to go solo as this was not serving me and I suspected it wasn't her either. I felt better for admitting it to myself. We can try and try and keep using our energies to make something work but after some advice from another business person, I realised it was better to let it go now. It would be messy and I felt pangs of guilt but I hadn't done anything wrong and felt unsupported. It came to a head one weekend towards the end of that year. Joe was in a crisis situation and I asked for support within the business. It was unmet and it was the final straw for me so I took action and terminated the business. I felt horrible and in a sea of the unknown and emotions but I knew in my heart it was the right thing to do. I had to honour my truth.

I picked my moments and never seemed to do things in halves as I had several clients all ready to have their books designed and published. I had a manic forty eight hours sourcing potential help and felt I had struck it lucky when I came into contact with a publishing graduate, someone out there was looking after me. I believe it was because I made the clear decision after hovering in an indecisive state for months and not feeling the best I could about the business set up. I then found another great person, again by *"chance"* to design book covers. After the initial chaos it worked out rather swiftly as it was meant to be. A few weeks later and all of the clients books were produced and delivered to their respective new authors. It was amazing and to have gone through the journey with them from scratch felt very special. It was a little bit like being a mum and nurturing the client.

Me being me, wearing my heart on my sleeve, I wanted to talk openly about Joe and how I was dealing, or not dealing with it but I kept quiet for his sake. I talked to my mum and close friends but longed to be more open and pictured myself talking and writing about it.

Joe got through the term, and before you knew it, Christmas was on our doorstep again.

18

Black Christmas

The last two or three Christmas's/New Year's, Joe and I have escaped the British winter climate for a week and escaped to one of the Canary islands which promises warmth and some sun rays for those months. This year we didn't sadly. A few reasons really, Joe was bogged down with lots of exam revision, he was also almost 20 and at that stage of wanting to holiday with mates, but mostly because of how he was feeling. As the years have passed, I have lost a lot of the childhood enthusiasm I had for the festive season. I think once your child gets older, plus going through a divorce it shakes life up, and I had got used to Christmas being with the family as ever but also of sunny climes. Christmas had begun to feel farcical in many ways with the materialistic world that we live in and the family naturally dwindling over the years with losing loved ones, it somehow was not the same, hence the desire for sunshine holidays!

By December I was a little tired from being very busy in the business and dedicating a lot of energy to that for months but also of worrying silently about Joe, only sharing a little with a friend and my mum. I've always been a worrier and I believe that to come from being highly sensitive and caring so damn much about people and principles of things in life that mattered a lot to me. I think the other stresses of the year caught up and got thrown into the mix also. Christmas is hyped up for months and even stepping back, you feel a certain amount of pressure to feel joyous and if you're not – something is wrong.

I'd been on a high prior to Christmas with creating several new authors and publishing a succession of amazing true stories and when I was on that plane, I didn't like coming off of it, that's some of my trouble, I never know when to stop – balance always being a desire. Passion is a powerful force and I loved nothing more than going full throttle with it, not always thinking of the consequences or ignoring that aspect at the time. Life was for living right? I wasn't as full on as I used to be prior to burning out before, as something within me would not allow that to happen, it was protecting me and the outside seasonal influences was indicating it was time to rest.

After starting to wind down from work, I surprised myself and started to feel excited about actual Christmas and not being away. I planned some fun stuff to do, including a spontaneous surprise extra gift to Joe, trekking with Alpacas followed by delicious mulled wine. We had family feasts lined up over the main days and some activities with friends.

My dear aunty Jean was very poorly around this time, as her cancer had cruelly returned and I made a few visits with my mum to see her, she was her sister in law. I was shocked to see her fast decline in health when we first visited the hospital ward, but Jean being Jean, put on a brave face and maintained her positive outlook. I felt for my cousin, Jean's daughter, a lot, as she had a young baby and a little boy.

Joe was relieved to have a break from the university workload but still had exam revision to do, but his anxiety symptoms were troubling him more than ever it seemed. To see your child in pain is really hard especially when there appears to be not one solution. Mental health being complex and is individual for each person. The only good thing I felt about it was that he openly talked to me, which is huge, and he knew that I understood him and was always there for him. It didn't feel enough to me! I wanted to rip his pain out and make it go away, my boy did not deserve this agony. For all I know about mental health after my own long journey, I was mad at myself for not being able to make him feel better sooner – pointless thinking I know, but unless you've been in that position, you have no idea of how heartbreaking it is. I especially attached so much to it as I had really tried to always encourage him to believe in himself and to be open, which he did. God I tortured myself and seemed to do it more when I was around him, and had to keep reminding myself that what I went through at his age is not the same for him and he wouldn't end up like I did. It scared me and kept me awake at nights.

We spent hours talking when he felt like it, I did some CBT type work with him and I urged him to try all of the things that can help. He said that his emotions felt stuck, and sometimes he wanted to cry in frustration rather than feeling sad. Maybe we tried too hard? I'm often guilty of that.

I felt myself slipping between feeling passion for my business, excitement for the Xmas activities and deep sorrow for Joe, quite a performance of emotions to contend with each day.

He had always insisted that he wasn't depressed as in-between the panic and anxiety, he was in good form and sprung back to Joe, even though going out socially had become a challenge and going to the gym became a no-no, as he was relating both events to panic attacks. That was one of the key points I explained to him, he was expecting the panic to take over and that expectation had enough emotion behind it to make it a reality, as your brain starts to look for reasons and evidence.

Christmas Eve arrived, the presents had all been wrapped and either given to the recipient or was under our tree. Well

I called it a tree, Joe jokingly called it a twig, as it was a modern day silver version of a tree. There had been a bit of a pickle over the booking of the alpacas trip so that was postponed until new year's eve now and so much for me keeping it as a surprise extra pressie – I only lasted a week as was dying to see Joe's reaction! I think it was a cross between unimpressed and bemused. I convinced him that we'd have a laugh and that it was healthy to try new experiences! His dad wasn't convinced either.

I had a bit of a lazy morning, not something I do very often, after a client call online. No rest for the wicked I hear you say, or maybe that's my soul speaking? We had my parents and brother coming over later on for a Christmas Eve supper followed by the present opening ceremony. Some years as Joe got older, we'd taken to this more continental tradition, my mum and dad had done it for years, since my brother and I were little, leaving Christmas morning for the children. In our family toilet humour (always guaranteed to have us in fits) Joe and I had wickedly wrapped up some surprise presents and placed them innocently under the tree, always the jokers. They were particularly wicked this year with the emphasis on realistic (but NOT real I hasten to add!).

A friend suggested we meet in town for a coffee and festive catch up, I loved the idea of being in the city centre on Christmas Eve, it added to the festive feeling. We don't live that far from town, a twenty minute pace and you're there. Joe decided to try the gym again and we walked in together. He seemed in a not too bad frame of mind and I invited him to join my friend and I after his session and he agreed to call me and see where we were. Two coffees, a good chat and several chocolates later, Joe rang but he didn't sound great in his voice. He'd decided to go home

– said he'd be okay and would see me later. I felt torn but he insisted that I stay on. We did a spot of last minute shopping, well my friend did. I was distracted with Joe on my mind a lot and began to feel an urge to get home as we were later in town than I'd planned on anyway – I still had a meal to prepare for tonight.

My friend dropped me home and when I got in, I went straight to see Joe and I could tell looking at him that he had not been in a great space. We chatted, he said he'd cried on the walk home from the gym and was feeling desperate for the anxiety to go away. My heart broke hearing him say those words and crumbled further when he revealed that he briefly considered doing something to stop it. Only for a second, but that was too much. The pain hit me deeply as I knew how he felt to even have that dark thought. I hugged him tightly and thanked him for trusting me and telling me and assured him that if he ever felt like that again he must speak to me. He cried a bit more and we were both a bit of an emotional mess for a few minutes. I told him how brave he was for managing these anxious feelings for several months now, that it was in no way a weakness but a show of strength of his character, even if he didn't believe that right now.

I remembered how weak it does make you feel inside but actually you are very courageous to battle those challenging feelings and thoughts. I now believe it to be the universe's way of sending you messages of certain areas of your life and yourself that you need to look at and possibly adjust. In my eyes, Joe had done brilliantly. He had never been any trouble all through his school years, he thrived on learning and was proud to be the top of his school. College was much the same but there were other very able students too. University had been a different kettle of fish. It was one of the top uni's also, where expectations were high and the students must feel the pressure. However, Joe had settled really well, which I know can be tough for a sensitive and more introverted person – he was far more settled and self confident than I'd been at his age. This past term had seen him take to more independent living, cooking many meals from scratch, looking after a joint house and the politics that can go with a household of different personalities. Not always easy! And of course, managing the work load. I learnt that it was common that students found it very stressful in their second year, when they had moved into shared accommodation and the work load ramped up. It made a lot of sense, and keeping it to myself, I wouldn't have given a thank you to spend a year living with people I didn't know that well. My idea of hell as a sensitive person!

I reminded Joe of all he had accomplished, not just academically but in his self development. He had said more than once *"mum, I think I'm finding out who I am"* which melted my heart each time as it sounded vulnerable yet wise at the same time. An old soul. We got ourselves together and decided to enjoy the evening with the family, after all we had the unveiling of the *"special gifts"* to come! I rushed into the kitchen and quickly knocked up the meal, a smoked paprika chicken stew, comfort food. I wasn't in the mood to cook at that point but needs must. My passion for cooking had long since passed, years of an eating disorder and the recovery tends to have that affect. I often used to have dinner parties and loved entertaining. These days, I preferred to be spending time relaxing and as a host I found that hard to do. It was a lovely meal all the same.

After dinner, my family were in festive spirits, I sort of was but had my recent conversation with Joe fresh in my mind, we sat down in a circle to unwrap our pressies. I loved this part. As soon as I unwrapped any chocolates, I ripped them open to sample, it was a Christmas tradition. I had a few drinks which helped me to unwind but Joe stayed teetotal, which was good. By the time my mum, dad and brother unwrapped their unsuspecting trick gifts, we were in hysterics, especially at their reactions and I loved seeing Joe laugh again. My dad was not as amused at what we had managed to create with melted chocolate and a pair of old boxer shorts, which encouraged the laughter. It took us ages to open all of our presents, as I insisted that we make it last and enjoy one another's company, it's all part of the ritual. Several more drinks later and it was heading towards midnight, and the family made their way home, we were back together again in just a few hours to my mums. Except Joe, he was at his dad's this year, we alternated that every Christmas, that was always a bit sad as he went off with his dad, especially when he was younger.

I tidied up empty glasses and strewn bits of wrapping paper and then Joe and I watched a comedy programme as we were not tired enough to sleep. He admitted that he had felt anxious most of the night, despite putting on a face.

19

A Christmas Like No Other

I must have been asleep for minutes when I heard Joe up and about. I switched on my light, glanced at my bedroom clock and it was only the early hours. Officially now Christmas Day.

I went to see what Joe was doing out of his bedroom and found him pacing about in a panicked state. My heart sank, as it struck me how different this year was in comparison to every other. I took one look at him and his face riddled in angst and asked him if he wanted to go for a walk? That may sound bizarre with it being the middle of the night, but it wouldn't be the first time and going for a walk really helped Joe to calm down. He took himself off for walks during the day sometimes when he was away in Nottingham. We bundled our thick coats on top of our nightwear, donned our shoes and went outside into the cold air. We walked around the streets for almost an hour, talking things through and rationalising his thoughts. There was no-one else around unsurprisingly, and you'd never think it was Christmas day looming with how we both felt. The brisk walk helped as usual, the physical sensations of anxiety died down, and the positive talking made us both feel more empowered to deal with the situation. We warmed up with the heating, then both went to our beds. Eventually I slept after my mind had been churning over and over.

Waking up a few hours later, it was the strangest, most unlike Christmas morning ever. With no presents to open, I took it easy, still feeling really tired from the exploits from the night. Joe was still asleep, and I let him sleep as long as possible before I knew he had to get up ready for his dad. Anxiety exhausts the life out of you with the adrenaline that gets released and swished around your physical body. He was not in a good frame of mind after last night and cried again. I felt such a failure – my grown son in tears on Christmas day. Yes it may sound harsh, but I'd always taken parenting seriously and it's a huge responsibility to decide to bring a child into the world, I'd always wanted the absolute best for him in order to lead a happy, healthy life; this wasn't it. I suspected some of my own old habits were sneaking back in a little as the last few months of supporting Joe had tired me out somewhat and felt as though I was shouldering most of the responsibility alone. I don't mean that in an angry tone at all, I was most grateful that Joe trusted in me and opened up regularly but I was only human too. I guess at times like this, being a single parent really struck home, with not having a partner to support me it was tough. I only wanted to talk to my mum or friends to a degree and felt that I'd already burdened them too much. Most of the time I just wanted a hug and someone to listen to me with no judgement. That meant a lot. I didn't want advice, unless it was from someone who really knew what they were talking about. Well-meaning advice had good intentions but it could also add to the stress load as it often wasn't relevant or was pushed upon you a little, or could even be damaging in a non-intentional way, holding space was far more helpful. Being hard on myself was what I'd apparently been a master at most of my life but I often failed to see it, these days I was pretty self-compassionate though and looked after myself on many levels. This wasn't normal circumstances however and there had been considerable other difficulties throughout the year that would have added to this moment. After trying not to cry for a long time, I found the tears falling. I wanted to roar my eyes out truth be told but didn't want Joe to witness that as I felt consumed with sadness. Always the protector, especially when it came to my son.

I gathered my thoughts and took charge of the situation. This was probably the worse state I'd seen Joe in and I decided I did not feel comfortable with him being away from me all day and overnight. He wasn't a baby, but he needed a mix of tough love, positive talk and compassion. I knew him, and when I voiced my thoughts to him, he agreed. I rang my dad to pick us up a little later and explained we'd have one extra mouth to feed and rang his dad to explain. I felt guilty for his dad when he came round, but he was understanding and saw how Joe was. He arranged to see him a little the following day instead. Both of us were shattered, and were trying to be cheery for the sake of my family but it was a real effort.

We went to my parent's local pub for Christmas drinks before lunch as we'd planned, and I felt more and more tense as the day went on. Seeing Joe with a lost look in his eyes haunted me and my energy was drained. By the time we'd had lunch and more conversation, I felt utterly miserable and overwhelmed wanting to cry. I was exhausted most of all. Joe's spirits in the meantime appeared to have picked up. I went to lay on my mum's bed and rested but couldn't sleep and cried a bit to myself. What a bloody Christmas; in that moment, I hated it. It's one of those times of year when you imagine the rest of the world to be happy and celebrating, even though that's far from the truth, its feels it all the same. Nothing like Christmas for making you feel lonely when life is not as you want it to be. It's no coincidence that the work of the Samaritans and other helplines are most in demand at this time of year. There's also the conflict of feeling alone but wanting to remain alone – where do you ever go with that?

I was still laying on my mum's bed when the phone rang and it was my aunty calling my mum. My aunty who was poorly. She had returned home but the situation was very difficult and her and my uncle were receiving support from Marie-Curie. From the conversation it sounded as though my aunty was on the up, and my mum confirmed this after she came off of the phone, I think she was surprised considering how ill my aunty was. Some good news today.

By the evening, I think both Joe and I were desperate for sleep.

20

Boxing Day

Although we were not out walking the darkened streets, Joe and I found ourselves with another middle of the night rendezvous as he experienced another state of panic which appeared to come to a peak when it was time to go to bed. We sat up talking, albeit in a tired manner and I gave him a mini coaching session – in an attempt to get him to empower himself again. We slept after this.

Boxing Day was more relaxed and we all congregated at my brother's house and yes for more eating and drinking! What with the disrupted sleep for two nights running and the overload of sugar and alcohol, I was shattered and slumped on a sofa most of the day quite happily, glad to be resting. My brother's cats joined us from time to time, demonstrating how different two personalities can be from the same family. One cat bigger and much friendlier and trusting, the other very petite, sweet and timid.

Joe avoided alcohol which was a good choice after we'd listed all of the things *"to do"* and *"not to do"* until this anxious stage had settled down for him. A combination of all of these separate actions can make such a difference overall:

- Healthy diet
- Regular exercise
- Keep talking, opening up
- Positive affirmations
- Deep breathing
- Meditation

- Being aware of energy – what is your own and what may be someone else's
- Listen to uplifting and empowering podcasts/videos
- Good sleep hygiene
- Writing down your feelings when they feel overwhelming
- Crying when you need to
- Not *"owning"* anxiety or other negative feelings as in *"I am"* or *"my anxiety"*
- Time to relax and rest
- Getting up to get motivated instead of sitting around
- Having structure in your day to give a sense of purpose and autonomy
- Spending time with supportive friends and family
- Reading helpful books
- Recognising when you have a negative thought and actively replacing it with a positive one

This list was not exhaustive but just what we compiled together. We tried other ideas out too, when I say *"we"* I don't mean always literally together, but I was always encouraging and supporting him, I knew how hard it was to lift yourself out of that space once it has taken hold and unhealthy habits have been formed. If a person could just *"pull themselves together"* or *"try harder to get better"* then I imagine most people on this planet would rather do just that than be in the place of ill mental health of any kind – as it really is a version of how you'd expect hell to be.

It was enjoyable all being together, despite the issues our family had lived through, we are now all pretty close and can actually have some damn good laughs in normal circumstances – outright crazy and stupid times in fact! If only those could see us behind closed doors! I guess it says a lot about the family members when a family can endure really bad struggles but still remain connected as a family, so many don't make it long term which always feels sad to me. However if some family members are too toxic then its best for everyone if there is separation and new habits can be then formed to pass onto new generations as all too often addictions and such like are repeated behaviours passed on and the cycle is never broken.

After a rather deliciously extravagant meal we watched some old family movies projected onto the lounges white wall. I loved looking back at these, especially to see Joe come to life on the film, hearing his cute little voice and looks when he was a toddler. Life passes us by so quickly, I treasure these memories with such love. It was hard to comprehend that the currently anxious teenager was once upon a time this happy little boy running around his grandma's garden getting up to all kinds of boyish adventures.

We slept well that night.

21

The End

A couple of days later I took the call to say that my aunty had passed away. I had gone out as needed to be out of the house for a while to clear my thoughts and energy and Joe was spending time with his dad. I was in a busy shopping centre of all places. It should not have been a shock really, as I knew how ill she'd been but it was a shock. I've never been able to get my head around the finality of death, right from being a young girl. Yes, I am one of those people in that it scares me. Some people seem at peace with the idea, I envy that. The speed at which my aunty's health declined had shocked us all I think but nothing does prepare you. I cast my mind back to just the other day and the phone call my mum had shared with her and how optimistic she had sounded. My heart went straight out to my uncle, they had been married for many years, my cousin and her children who were very young. It's hard enough to understand and accept death as an adult but how are children meant to grasp it?

Tears were pricking, so I hurried myself off to a café to gather my thoughts. There was such sadness surrounding me at the moment, it felt overwhelming as an empath. I needed to protect myself more efficiently as us highly sensitive souls feel all of it. I sat for a while and let thoughts pass through me until I felt stronger and an urge that came to me was that I wanted to join a gym. Not sure where that came from as I am no gym bunny that's for sure, it takes hell of a lot of motivating to get me into a gym as I find those environments unsettling. I think my higher self was speaking to me and encouraging me to take action on something very different for me, that had always been a challenge given my past history and that I would obtain strength from this activity. I felt a buzz of excitement when I considered it and taking some rather radical action always excited me.

The period between Christmas and New Year, or Twixmas as it's been labelled in recent years, always seemed a strange time, with nothing much happening and no real sense of normality. I don't respond well to times like this and always feel stressful emotions rising within. It reminds me of my eating disordered days which were utter chaos with no structure and what seemed like masses of endless time to while away. Empty time used to stress me out more than anything and my binges often used to be triggered by this. Diving deeper into that, I can see now how I was unable to sit with feelings and any kind of discomfort, hence me feeling this deep emptiness and always trying to fill it with outrageous food binges or alcohol, or relationships, or the latest obsession. Always on some sort of a mission and any sign of boredom making me run for the hills! All learnt from a very young age. Similar could be said these days, I am very driven and one of the most self-motivated people I know (hello Sam!), but I recognise the big difference these days though, is that my drive is full of positive purpose which is very different in comparison. I try to be mindful not to work too much as that itself is an addiction and just another way of not dealing with emotions. But I feel purposeful when I perform my daily tasks and deliver my passions. It makes me content and that is gold. Sure there are frustrations, and that's usually when I'm wanting things to go faster. Back to the same subject I guess, of not wanting to sit still. I do though, I rest quite a lot these days and this is why my thoughts of the gym were even more unexpected!

We got together for a family meal at my mums with my uncle, cousin and her family as a comfort for them at this incredibly sad time, I wanted to hug them all better. A week or so later, we gathered for my aunty's funeral followed by the wake. It felt comforting in a sad sort of way, being together as a family. She was such a lovely caring person.

22

The Word Was Epic

I was hugely relieved for the New Year to begin after the heaviness of the Christmas season, I had set myself some pretty big goals for my business and for other areas of my life. Last year, when I looked back at my written goals in an end of year challenge I did with a friend, I'd reached practically all of them, which always felt so good!

For the first time ever, I set myself a word for the year – EPIC! That was the kind of year I desired.

I wanted to put this sadness behind me, not in a callous way, but to seek what I knew was there for me and my family. Joe's main Christmas present from me was a short break away in Oxford – with me! We may not have got abroad this time but was determined to spend some time away and quality time, we both more than deserved a break. It was in the first week of January for two nights in a lovely hotel. I envisioned us doing it in style too, not on the cheap as in years gone by to tap into my feelings and vision of abundance and manifestation. We did have a lovely time away, with luxuries – taxi travel, nice meals out, time in the hotel pool and spa but it was also laced with more panic attacks for Joe. My heart went out to him and I hated seeing him tortured by his own mind. We stopped at one point in a café so he could plug in his earphones and meditate as his panic sensations took him over. Sometimes he seemed more like the Joe I knew and other times, it was as though a different person had been placed into his body. I was always aware that I was picking up on his anxious vibrations and tried to put some distance between us energetically and remain strong and upbeat for both of us. I'd come to realise in life that it's all about the energy, if you think negatively, you feel negatively and you attract negatively with those vibes. The great news is that you can reverse that and attract great things into your life.

When Joe returned to university he had the pressure of exams looming over him so I urged him to reach out for support from the staff. He did this, but also found the stress overwhelming with how he was already feeling. There was one time in January, I was working in a café, feeling pretty sorry for myself (not a luxury I allow myself very often!) As I had some type of flu which was draining me but one of my clients had invited me to her book launch that evening, so I dosed myself up and got on with it, I wouldn't have missed it for the world. Sitting in Nero's, tucked away in a corner, attempting to concentrate through a head fog so thick you needed headlights to see anything, aches and shivers all over my body and a constant streaming nose, I felt bloody miserable. Every time I'm ill, which luckily is not very often, I swear blind I won't take my health for granted again, but I do. Naughty really, as once we don't have it, boy do we notice it. Then my phone rang, it was Joe.

At the end of the line, I just knew instinctively, it wasn't going to be good news. As he began to speak, I could feel his anxious vibes through the phone and his voice was not his. That anxious alien had taken over again to the point where he'd taken himself out for a long walk at Wollaton Park which was adjacent to his uni campus in Nottingham. He was feeling distressed with the physical symptoms of fight or flight to the degree of considering not attending his exam in around three hours time. I mostly talked, feeling I sounded like a recorded meditation message especially designed for him and after about an hour's call he had calmed down significantly and enough to attend his exam. Phew. Every time we had one of these calls, my motherly instinct was to rush over there and protect him and wrap him in my arms like he was a baby again and soothe him. Learning to soothe yourself is vital, as I'd discovered in my adulthood and why I tried to empower him to learn all of these skills for himself. Having the fully equipped emotional toolbox makes for an extremely smoother ride in this adventure known as life.

He let me know that he'd been and done his exam later on, I could have cried with how proud I was of his strength. That put me in a much more positive head-space, knowing he was better, and an improved frame of mind to attend Tracey's book launch, even with tissues and pills galore! It was a wonderful evening, you could tell she was an event organiser with the attention to detail and beautiful setting she had created. She had a very supportive turn out and I sat listening, and again, felt that sense of pride at what Tracey had achieved. She had decided through writing about her story, that she felt a deeper purpose and a desire to help others in bereavement as she had experienced and on the back of her book, she was setting up a foundation. Now that is what I call purpose and felt blessed to have been a part in her journey. By the time I got home close to midnight, I was done for and promised myself a day of rest the following day.

The next couple of months were busy, working with new clients and new ideas manifesting, it was such an exciting path I was on - one never knew what may happen next!

Alongside Joe, I also had a friend going through a really rough time. Her story reminded me a lot of how I'd been years before, in and out of jobs, not settling and finding it distressing just to live each day. I saw clearly now, how being this highly sensitive person was a massive contributing factor as place that person with hyper vigilance to sounds, tones, moods, and a number of other subtleties, never mind outright toxic behaviour into the wrong environment and they will suffer with the overload of feelings, emotions and the thoughts created around those. Seeing her tears, it felt as though they could have been mine as I can remember how harrowing those times had been. We met up for coffees and chats and I know that was hard for her to do.

From time to time, I would check out various people I was connected with on Facebook but didn't really see, to see what they were up to and how they were. One of these people was a girl, now a woman in her forties, who had been at Chester Lodge with me as a teen. She had found me on Facebook a couple of years previously and we'd spoke of meeting up with another friend from there, Vicki, who I mentioned in my first book, but it never actually happened. For some reason, I felt compelled to go to her page that day as I knew that she still struggled with herself greatly. My heart almost stopped as I was stunned to read a post her husband had put on a few months previously, around the time of my birthday. She had passed away. It didn't give details but I was convinced it was from on her ongoing battle with an eating disorder and the serious consequences of that, she had caused a lot of damage to her kidneys with the abuse they'd been subjected to for decades. It shocked me to the core as she was around my age, had been in the unit at the same time as me and yet despite her battle, she was no longer here. That could have been me and was always a worry when I was bulimic. However, I also knew that the struggle with self was so powerful it was not enough to deter me either to stop the behaviours when my self-esteem was on the floor.

It probably sounds crazy to an observer, but unless you have walked the path of an addiction, especially an eating disorder, you have no idea of what it takes to release yourself.

The big issue with an ED is that you cannot quit your *"drug"*, you have to eat to survive and therefore make friends somehow with your addictive substance. It's somewhat a torment and an eating disorder, particularly Anorexia, is the highest cause of death out of all mental illnesses. Bloody hell, I realised in that moment, just how lucky I was to be alive. After a quick calculation, (I find stuff like this powerful to do!) I reckoned that I'd put my body through the repulsive cycle of bingeing and purging (throwing up for me) in the region of over 13,000 times in sessions (the amount of actual times of being sick many, many more). That shocked me even further and wondered how I actually was still alive and healthy to boot. I would not return to those dark days for anything, they were a living hell, yet also a comfort in a sickened way at the time. The devil you know and another reason it was so tremendously challenging to free yourself from the evils of an ED.

It took the birth of my son, after all, and my undying love for him to have a strong enough desire to get well and kick my habit. If Joe had not arrived in my world, god knows where I'd have been, as back then, I was not the person with the mindset I have today. I was always determined and convinced there had to be a happier life but inside I felt so weak and powerless, but most of all, unworthy; the catch of not feeling deserving to not creating change. Many stay in that place which is just too awful to think about. I think my old friend was one of these people and she did not deserve the life she had.

All of this plus losing my aunty, propelled me into taking action on a new idea – I hated to feel dis-empowered, especially as a mum to Joe and I needed a way to channel this energy into something so positive it would outshine this sadness around me. One bus journey to Loughborough for a meeting with my new typesetter later, and the idea was born.

23

Courage: Stories Of Darkness To Light

Collaborative books appeared to be on trend with many compilations doing the rounds, the majority of them seemed to focus on empowering women and entrepreneurial women. These were interesting but they didn't excite me to my core – I was always fascinated by struggle, overcoming adversity and what was underneath a persona, the raw vulnerable person, and not necessarily exclusively women either. We as a universe are made up of souls of both sexes and of a completely diverse range of backgrounds, cultures, religions and experiences. My idea had to represent that and as with my first book, the title came to me with ease. I'd actually mentioned the *"darkness to light"* a year or two ago in a social media post, which showed up recently on my Facebook memories, so this was already in the bud of creation without my realising that at the time.

Arriving early at the café in Loughborough, I decided to just take immediate action after doing my sums on the bus and figuring out the how to. Without another thought, I whipped my phone out of my bag, and sitting in a quieter space, I launched a Facebook live. Sharing my book idea and my passion, I didn't hold back and immediately received traction and enquiries from people. I was amazed at how quickly the responses were which showed me just how many people out there do want to share their story. The book sales were to be donated to The Samaritans, I'd always wanted to give back to them after the unlimited non-judgemental support they provided me as a teen, when I was beside myself. I don't know what I'd have done without them there. There was a low cost to cover some of my time and the creation of the book and I wanted to put together a collection of powerful true stories of mental health struggles from people of all walks of life, to represent all different types of ill mental health and how it can happen to anyone at any time. We also were going to share what helped them through that time in their lives. Wow, this was going to be one special book!

Within a couple of days or so I had sixteen people lined up who were committed to the book project and almost enough interest to create a second book, I was blown away. Not long after this I launched the mentoring to support the short story writing. I asked Joe and my friend if they wished to contribute and explained how they had inspired me to do this. Neither felt they could at that time as they were still struggling which I understood. It's hard when you are depressed and / or anxious to concentrate to read never mind write or to have the drive to want to do it.

The contributing authors were amazing – all with completely different stories and struggles – perfect for this purpose. We had men, women, different ages, from different countries, different cultures – exactly what the book stood for and the commonality throughout was COURAGE. They were brave bad-asses! They survived what they did and were now sharing that to help others – if that's not courageous I don't know what is. I was so proud to be working with them and guiding them through this journey of book creation.

Joe's journey was changing by the week, and all depended on what was happening in his world. I was very proud of him of taking stance on becoming more assertive in his life, something that had been lacking a little. Once we get into the habit of pleasing others and of not putting our own needs first (yes, society has loved to condition us on this being a selfish habit) we lose ourselves, little by little and eventually end up feeling rubbish, feeling angry and resentful but not sure why and how we reached that destination. I knew these layers all too well and was still in the progression of removing some of my people pleasing habits. If he could make this a habit now, it would serve him well in years to come.

Throughout life there will always be people and situations that will arise to challenge us, they will make us question ourselves and hopefully, make us look within to see if there is something we need to adjust. Knowing how to manoeuvre through these experiences and of how to protect your energy as an empathic person, is of paramount importance. It's easy to dismiss ourselves as *"weak"* when we don't feel ourselves, but as I frequently reminded Joe, weakness doesn't come into it, you are stronger than you'll ever know for living through these times no matter how much you feel you are falling apart. Breakdown can lead to breakthrough.

Alongside being assertive, is boundaries, and we examined these too. I knew I'd always had some issues surrounding setting enough of these to protect myself because of my own upbringing, and habits learnt. I might not have always been the best teacher for Joe when I was younger, as I was still working through my own trials but my undoubting love and loving intention had always been evident, I knew that and he had always felt it. This might all sound rather *"coachy"* to some people reading this, in our mum and son relationship, but I guess our own experience is what shapes us. I love coaching and mentoring, and self-coaching to find our best outcomes and wanted to support Joe in finding his.

It was interesting on how the boundaries topic had arisen as I was soon to receive a series of nasty shocks, later perceived as lessons in this. The beauty of hindsight.

24

The Good, The Bad and The Ugly

Just after I had written my first book, and that truly magical week where it all came together via the universe, with many extra gifts attached, life was never the same again…well I recently I experienced another week like that, but even better!

If I step back and pause, my mind is blown at how far I have come, but the part of this that truly takes some getting my head around, is that it has all just come to me, literally, no effort involved. I want to try and put together what has happened as this is life changing. This week proved to me that it IS possible. As you may gather from my story, my past traumas and so on, it plunged me into a mindset of survival. Now survival is not a good place to be, as like attracts like and it's so easy to fall into the loop consistently attracting drama, of incidents and people that do not serve your highest self.

Over the two weeks prior to this specific week, I had some pretty dismal experiences after life had been going along tickety boo. Someone relatively close to me, chose to share with me about someone I know, something that was rather disturbing which a few years before would have greatly upset me, as the sensitive soul that I am. However, although it made me think, I saw it for what it was, her belief, not mine. Big difference right?! Then her behaviour became more unusual as some other beliefs came tumbling out. I didn't judge, although they were hard to get my head around but went with it. However, it then turned sour. The person decided not to pay me for some work that I had done for her which created ill feelings as you could imagine. But here is the difference, rewind a year or two ago, I would have fought tooth and nail for what was mine, the money I had earnt. This time, as sick as I felt, I sat with the emotions, allowed myself to feel them, then quickly detached myself energetically from the person and the situation. How did I do this? I spoke about it to release it, I observed what had happened and saw that there had been some little signs that I had ignored along the way.

Instead of dumping all of the blame onto myself, the habit that has greatly not served me most of my life, I acknowledged that there was a signed contract, this was not about my wrongdoing. For once, I was not going to feel bad and guilty and allow it to be transferred onto me, leaving me questioning myself for months, possibly years to come. Neither was I set to fight, as fighting creates huge resistance and I didn't want that either. I chose to let it go; wow, let it go. The one thing that had challenged me the most of all throughout my life in many settings, was detaching. This was because of several factors: I felt deeply, I was determined - bordering on stubborn and had a keen sense of justice.

Don't get me wrong, it took a few days to properly release and settle, but I stood by it and it dispersed. Amazing. That in itself was huge for me, HUGE!

A couple of days passed by and ping, I experienced an online troll. It took me quite by surprise as she landed on my profile page, I felt the underlying intention but responded amicably. She continued to progress more aggressively and it wasn't pleasant to experience but again, I deflected it from me as I knew it was her story, not mine to keep. *"At long last Sam"*, I heard my higher self exclaim, *"you're finally getting it!"* I broke away and detached myself from the person. It left me a little bewildered as I had done nothing to provoke her but she was clearly suffering within.

The following day, I had another experience. Yes it was quite a week! A different person, and I found that I was having to explain myself, until I thought, no I don't have to do that, I don't have to justify myself to anyone. That's another old belief that I'm no longer prepared to hold onto. Fortunately, this all resolved itself as the person wasn't horrible towards me, misunderstanding maybe, and she came back to me a few days later to apologise, as someone had just rejected her and she was reeling from the shock and hurt. That was humbling and made me wonder just how many times in life that had actually been the case? Someone had been hurt and took it out on someone else? You can see how chaos is created.

Two days, troll lady was back, this time on my Facebook business page, two clicks later and she was removed. I felt the boiling rage from her through the internet, all the way from the USA. Then another *"spiritual troll"* showed up to test me. Again, they didn't appreciate a polite response and attempted to put me down further. It's amazing really when this happens, as there you are minding your own business, sharing your truth on your own personal space in the online world, all done with good intention and by most people's feedback, I kept a very positive and upbeat page. Some people cannot stand this however and because of how bitter they are inside themselves they find it impossible to stay out of your business and with nothing positive to contribute, they do the opposite and attack. Commonly referred to as *"haters"* these days, not a term I like, but if the cap fits…

My energetic self obviously didn't brush this off as much as I thought I had with fragments lingering in my mind, as this was only the start of a series of a combination of some bad business decisions, a whole lot of heartache, and a considerable loss of earnings. The nightmare three months were only just getting warmed up and I wanted to share the contrast of being in a fantastic place of attracting great opportunities and people into my business and life to the Law Of Attraction continuing to work but now my mindset was not where it was, affected by these unpleasantries. I questioned how I had begun to attract more and more of these things I did not desire. Please remember, like attracts like, you are the guide to the vibrational energy you are putting out there.

Dumbly, ignoring my initial intuition, I signed up to work with a business/mindset coach, always wanting to take my business to the next level to impact more lives. Recommended by the client who refused to pay me earlier, I had investigated this coach and my first instincts were that although it was powerful what she was teaching, I did not like her energy. It felt an aggressive vibe on some level, and there was something I wasn't quite sure about; she was intimidating. So there was Sam, reverting back to old tricks, thinking something along the lines of *"oh I must have got that wrong, look at the results she's getting for people…Let me watch some more webinars and see what I think then."* Second chance right there, after that strong instinct to stay away. Why, Sam why? My higher self must have been thinking – what the hell! Younger version of Sam stepping in, the doubtful girl, the one who didn't believe in herself and allowed herself to be manoeuvred around like a pawn on a chessboard by all and sundry, each time her true self sinking further into an abyss of protective layering.

A week or so later, a very brief online conversation with the above mentioned coach and a good chunk of money dished out on a credit card, I was signed up for this programme.

Immediately, I was bombarded with masses of emails. I'd never had so many at once and nearly all of them were trying to sell me onto something else already. It didn't stop with my in-box though as the barrage of up-sells came through Facebook messenger too. That started making me feel a little overwhelmed already, and miffed that I had not benefited yet from this programme, so don't sell to me again already. Where is the integrity in that? I logged onto the portal online and it was vast, the content was intense and I was totally overwhelmed. Just in the first module were many videos, some almost 3 hours each plus lots and lots of downloads and worksheets to work my way through. If I could have parked my business for a month or two and focussed 100% on this I may have stood a chance, but I did not have that luxury currently. By the time I'd got through one lengthy training there was another, plus loads more emails and messages with new information to take action on.

The pile of overwhelm amassed, I'd never experienced *"learning"* like it. I felt like I was failing before I'd begun. There were also live calls to take part in and two Facebook groups – yikes! The aspect that stood out to me most of all though, was the energy within the whole set up. I didn't like it, not one bit, yet I tried to make myself like it as I'd invested in this and would be paying for it for another twelve months, but was under a four month pressure to get it all done – that is, if you wanted their support - and it was vast. After a week or so, I reached out and expressed how much I was struggling with it. It did not feel aligned and the actual content was bewildering and not suited for me as I was questioning them about at the beginning. I was happy with my programmes as they were, they were simple and easy to follow, (I love simplicity) and had many clients now go through my programmes successfully. I didn't want to change them up with lots of fancy words that didn't ring true to me or add tiers of up-sells and such like. It confused me so much.

I was contacted sporadically but with little understanding and in the end, the actual coach herself became very aggressive when I said that I wanted to leave, after I removed myself from her Facebook groups because the energy repelled me. She was manipulative and demanded that I pay her $1000 Australian dollars to leave. This was nowhere in the contract – in fact there was no contract. I immediately knew what my intuition had felt and had communicated to me. That energy, it never lies, so please take heed of this, and it was the lesson I obviously still needed to fully trust in, embrace and honour to myself from now on going forwards.

In the end I blocked her on Facebook as she was horrible, she said she wasn't angry but I felt her rage. I am very sensitive to anger and for all the people that claim they are not angry when their actions speak otherwise – I call you out on the bullshit now. I went into my default fear and felt really threatened; something in my past had created this and was still triggered when I relived a similar experience. I spoke to my credit card company and they eventually were able to help me to cease future payments.

That clearly was not enough of my life lessons quota as the next week there were two more little incidents. The next day I was exhausted, and a few days later I was calmer again and hoped everything would all settle down.

Then last but not least, there was another angry person. Again, denying such feelings but clearly so with their totally unreasonable demands. I grew up around some angry feelings and if nothing else, I am finely attuned to others' feelings of anger. It makes me sick and I cannot sleep and worries me like nothing else. An old trigger for sure, but that's what made it so powerful that week as I managed to move beyond most of them without too much scarring. That for me, is in itself, a mini miracle. Then, being able to detach on top so that I was able to return to my good vibes is mind blowing. I am so grateful universe for teaching me these lessons, I think I finally nailed them! (If you've read my first book you'll totally understand where I'm coming from!).

So I guess you are now wondering where this magical week is hiding?

25

Magic

"The magic week amongst the chaos. The great week camouflaged in the other eleven weeks of mostly stress."

This statement, makes it seem all the more special, and so many blessings and lessons to learn, so let me try and explain it to you, as I know the universe was shouting loudly at me for several weeks running, just like it did when I put pen to paper in 2017.

Okay, so from someone I had never met, I was asked to run a writing retreat, in Scotland. Now that was exciting and I immediately felt drawn to partake. It was this kind of synchronicity that astounded me and made me revel like a kid at Christmas!

Then I began with a new ghost-writing client, again, we had never previously had a connection and he wanted a 5 book deal! Can you imagine how amazing this felt?

I started with 4 new clients in a short space of time, had oodles of fresh enquiries and then to put the cherry on the top, the medium secure psychiatric unit I had a relationship with responded very positively to a suggestion of a couple of ideas I had put to them.

What a week!

What did I do differently to take me from the negative mindset I'd slipped into to this abundant, magnificent state? I stopped trying as hard. Yes really, which for me was not my regular go to strategy but to be fair to myself, I was changing and adopting to working with ease over the last two years, but this was incredible manifestation. A therapist had advised me a few years ago to stop trying as hard, I didn't even recognise in myself that I did, or not to the extent that burnt me out. She said that it was like I was consistently prodding myself to do more, and when I had done more, to do even more than that. Yes I can relate to the whole *"high achiever"* and *"imposter syndrome"* train of thoughts but it was a surprise to me to have this pointed out so bluntly. So this may explain the magnitude towards this whole letting go that I was embracing more and more.

Detaching, by knowing you have no control of what happens outside of yourself so why even try, and that the more you take on invisible faith, the more you get to let go. Letting go created space and when you did this, you made room for more abundantly beautiful things to rock on in. Or, if your mind was not focussed on the positive, you could find yourself with stuff you don't want. I had also learnt that you must remain unattached to the outcome of what you desire, and embody the feeling of already having it, rather than not having it. It's kind of like tricking your mind into believing something that will serve you – all while your inner critic will try to sabotage that – you can see the challenge and why it doesn't pan out in a great way for most people. Oh yes, and to also be open to receiving that what you asked for. Maybe it might be packaged a little differently to what you expected, but if you can trust that at all times our universe is working for you and not against you (I know how it can feel this way, I really, really do!), you'll be winning!

This portion of my life demonstrates this and the power of The Law Of Attraction so clearly and how when we are able to focus on abundance and not come from lack, we receive the greatness. It will also provide evidence to see how easy it can be to flip right out of that state and back into lack, and that the underlying message is to master our thoughts.

26

Flipping Out of Abundance

In the midst of this period I had also embarked on a getting fit project, remember what I'd felt at the end of last year and my gym aspirations? Well, after being inspired by a friend and her efforts, I joined a gym challenge with another friend with similar goals as me. It was tough, but started off well and I was very pleased with myself for sticking to it. I'd lost a stone and a half last year but some of this had found its way back onto my frame. Seems I still had not learnt my lessons here in that diets do not work, especially extreme cutting back. A few weeks in, and I became very stressed – finding it hard to juggle my workload and keep this commitment up and I refused to succumb to remove all carbs from my diet for the purpose of the challenge.

The more I became embroiled, the more triggering and unhelpful it was to me and I had stark reminders of my eating disordered days, becoming obsessive about what I weighed and that all important number on the scales. Crazy – I could not put myself through it and pulled away, this was not meant for me. I had to focus on balance, especially when it came to my food intake. It may have worked for some people but it wasn't serving me and I was doing the right thing for Sam. Still wanting to get fitter, I joined a different gym, that focussed on exercise only and with quite a bit of resistance initially, I gradually eased myself into regular classes, two or three a week, and I maintained it. I cannot say I looked forward to it, but I half enjoyed it when I was there and loved myself afterwards for doing it. I focused on the after feelings and this spurred me on to keep turning up for classes.

I saw Joe as often as I did when he was away at uni, some weekends I'd go there and sometimes he'd return home. I kept trying to support him, but sometimes during these few months I found it harder than ever as I felt low myself. In the end I had a one off session with a counsellor to ensure I was doing the best actions to support him, and I was doing most of the things. It also confirmed to me that I was well connected to Joe and his needs. I knew some of my own suffering was because I also decided to dump a lot of mum guilt on myself and often cried at how I had failed Joe. I felt real raw guilt and almost convinced myself his pain was mostly down to me. Where exactly had Sam gone? Because this wasn't her.

It demonstrates clearly I feel, that no matter how much personal development work you have invested in yourself, that an excess of external pressures all in a short time frame, plus an individual's personality and maybe other factors can become too much – even for the brightest, most positive person at times. We are all human with basic human needs, that if not met for prolonged periods, will create a certain amount of disarray. The fact that I'd already spent far too much of my life in a dark hole or desperately trying to climb the slippery walls out of one was always a massive motivator for me, to the point that most days of my life, part of my visualisations would be *"away from"* and I'd disappear into the imagery of me as a teenager, imprisoned (by myself) in my bedroom wanting to not be here anymore. Or of being on a psychiatric ward for the umpteenth time – and the hellish experience that is.

It may sound bizarre – but that actually injects rocket fuel into my being like nothing else! It makes me want to run as far away as possible to escape to be the person I had always aspired to be one day, one day in the very distant future that I could only just picture. No longer fuelled by shame, thank god, I'd let that heavy burden go finally, I used my past pain as a purpose and was very distressed to be back in a lower space, even if it was human. That's the thing I came to discover, that I panicked like crazy if I felt low for a few days – I was always a bit fearful of it being a warning sign of worse things. The more conscious part of me knew that wouldn't help as I'd attract more worry but that's the paradox of being a human right there. I just did what I always did and got on with it. Strangely enough, I was still doing well in my business and attracting opportunities but then again, I had learnt to focus like a laser on that part of my world.

My energy was not as it was obviously with my vibration, and electrical items around me decided to stop working – one after another, creating a considerably expensive two months. First up was the microwave which actually set itself on fire a little scaring the hell out of me, swiftly followed by the washing machine – stopping while full of water never to work again. I think the online electrical store thought they were onto a good thing at this point…only about 4 weeks later, the oven just stopped heating up, just like that. It gave me shivers.

The charity book project– Courage: Stories Of Darkness To Light was gaining momentum as the collaborating authors stories began to appear in my in-box for editing. I felt an immense feeling of being proud of them all for their big hearted bravery. A few of the original line up had bowed out but that is the very nature of what I do, fear or lack of focus sets in for some more than others.

Meanwhile, a disturbing experience evolved, that proceeded to knock me for six, triggered by something I said. The situation escalated quickly and appeared to be the opening for some beliefs that had secretly been felt about me to be unleashed. I observed the projection of what they felt about themselves onto me, I felt the force of the anger. I felt sick to the stomach and the fear was building up inside of me, my heart threatening to pound so hard it would burst through my chest.

Shock took over. Maybe I had got this all very wrong and there was no ill intention here? But hang on, if that was true, why did I feel this way. And why was Sam doubting herself when she knew what she was feeling? I shared some of the conversation with a friend to check in with *"am I over-thinking this and getting it very wrong?"* Er no, most definitely not according to my friend who was furious at the words said to me.

It was a bonus that this happened on a gym day as I power walked to the actual gym in record time – amazing what anger does and how powerful it can be when channelled for good purpose. I was that angry I dissolved into some tears during the gym class, then was advised to use the punch bag – I did with a little relief! That night, the feelings of fear increased intensively. I usually slept like a well fed baby, but that dark night I tossed and turned and had two hours sleep, because my palpitations were so fierce I couldn't sleep through them and was very on edge, with that feeling that something very bad was foreboding. I strongly felt betrayal, disbelief and shock most of all I felt sick and the next day was exhausted and could barely function.

The next few weeks were incredibly difficult for me as more bad feelings towards me unfolded. I cried most days and plunged into a very low place, finding it increasingly challenging to take the thoughts out of my head and the fear in my heart. I felt all of my personal power had drained away and I cocooned myself into a state of being like a scared child. I was shocked at my own behaviour but I felt powerless against it, not by conscious choice I hasten to add, I found it impossible to shift. I was mad with myself for not rising above it all, but the feeling of shock consumed my being.

Clearly triggering some past wounds in me, an emotional flashback brought a school scenario to the forefront and how my best friend had spread nasty rumours about me at school and all the other kids abandoned me.

That raw immense feeling of being blamed took me right back to my teenage years. It also reminded me very much of how I'd felt then behaved about 10 years ago when I experienced sexual abuse in my workplace.

That too was intolerable as my power felt sucked out of me, desperately not wanting to be a victim. Friends noticed the change in me and were surprised as I was not myself and they had never seen me like this before. In order to somehow deal with this, I wanted to equip myself with education on how to best sort this mess out and move on.

As usual it helped me enormously to read and hear about other people's experiences – it instantly made me feel comforted and knew I was not alone with these awful feelings.

This is where I gained much more clarity on what I was experiencing, taking on board what was going on. As I educated myself further, I realised the worst part of this was the level of confusion I was feeling after what had been said to me.

I continued with the daily internal conflict of wanting to get on with my life as I had been, thriving, and just standing up and blocking off what had been said to me as I didn't consider it to be true to now feeling like a little child, too scared to do anything and wanting to hide from the world. The old wounds were keeping me back.

27

Escape To The Sea

My business pages were trolled and it was most distressing, my impulse was to respond and I did, to start with, in a non-argumentative manner, but I seemed to make it worse. The more I educated myself the more I followed the advice. I blocked this person from my pages A friend spotted what was going on and stood up for me, as did I but I felt weak as a baby lamb inside. I enrolled on a self-help programme as I was desperate to free myself of this questioning myself and doubting my truth. I realised then, that this had happened before, several times in my past and really did tip you upside down and inside out.

The effects became so much that I slipped into feeling disassociated, which if you've experienced this is horrible. When you feel traumatised, it's your mind's way of attempting to protect you and it's as though you are on another planet and cannot think clearly at all. It became almost impossible to work, and all I wanted to do was read and watch videos to help free myself. It may sound over the top to read about, and how much it affected my mindset, but unless you have ever experienced this nothing could prepare you for the manner in which this sneaks in and monopolises your mind before you are fully aware.

I tried all kinds of things to help initially, including things that held no belief for me but I would have tried anything at that point. I carried around crystals to protect my aura, I performed cord cutting rituals over and over, I slept with some herbs for psychic attack under my pillow, I grounded myself outside, I saged my home, I had salt baths, I did meditations, I wrote a letter then burnt it to release the energy. It was exhausting.

I picked up an excellent book I have about trauma and CPTSD and knew this incident had triggered all kinds of old memories within me. I was able to be clear about this and separated them from what was happening now and understood why it got so deep under my skin, it would be unpleasant to most people I imagine but it had re-traumatised me to an extent, and why I couldn't just snap out of it. I had to work through a lot of things. I understood now that flashbacks didn't have to be just visual as I dismissed that I had them, always making me rule out CPTSD but they could actually be emotional and still considered a flashback. I definitely had these – going into my old school, going to old areas of my life brought me to tears thirty years later. I gave myself a lot of self-compassion. I continued reading and watching masses of videos and it was these that really helped me to start moving through it and speaking with a friend that had been through this experience really helped me to see it wasn't just me it was happening to as I felt so isolated with it.

You could say things in this period peaked when I reached my absolute limit as they couldn't seem to help themselves from reattaching to me. Talking online had got us nowhere so I took a deep breath and contacted them and suggested we have a phone call, following my instinct on how to make peace with this situation as I couldn't go on any longer. One very surreal phone call later shocked me further at the intensity of their outburst but I persisted as needed closure. Joe heard some of it and was shocked too and he hugged me afterwards as I cried. My movements online had been watched and the whole situation freaked me out. I put off my meeting later that day as I was shaken up and kept crying.

More shock. How exactly did I get that so wrong? I felt a fool at not seeing this coming. I did ask myself why I was allowing this to affect me so much and reminded myself of all of the work I'd done on myself; I obviously still needed to do more work on my self-belief. It's actually common in business, to feel a fraud and part of imposter syndrome and is the reason why business owners have to work a lot of self-development, as ego loves to try and trip us humans up and convince us to stay small. In psychology there is also a term called the *"Dunning-Kruger"* effect, which when learning about this recently, helped me to put into proportion the whole self-belief and fraud feeling too and see it for what it really is. For example, when people find a specific thing easy, for example, writing for me, they underestimate their ability because of its ease. Therefore coming to the conclusion that *"ah it's easy, it can't be that good,"* bringing up feelings of being a fraud, then labelling self and forming a new belief. Recognise this in yourself? Plus we get conditioned to believe that for something to be worthy it must be a struggle…madness!

All areas of my life were affected as I went deeply further into a mass of confusion and disbelief and struggled to release myself. I spent further money on an energy healing session and a coaching session, purely to free myself of this as it felt as though I had a dark mass of bad energy attached to me that wouldn't budge and was invading my mind and body. The sessions helped a little but not enough to stop me from crying. I invested further in an online course and an ebook and kept reading and pouring over videos. They made me feel stronger and gradually began to give me more of a sense of understanding. I wanted to be better equipped to deal with this type of person going forwards as I had experienced more than my fair share over the years.

I would implement any changes that I needed to and give

myself even more self-compassion and Love. I tried to keep this away from others, especially Joe, as much as possible but it was hard when I was in that emotional state. Some days I could be like a zombie because I had been so distressed and the brain fog was hideous; that horrible helpless feeling as you keep trying and trying to pull yourself up but then slip back down. Shame began to creep up on me from keeping it mostly to myself and there was no way on earth I was prepared to go down that road again. I didn't put a tag-line of *"A Secret Life"* in my first book for nothing. Dark secrets breed shame and shame is probably one of the most damaging emotions you can feel as it destroys your self esteem and self-belief.

I joined some online groups for mutual support.

Doubting yourself, second guessing what you've done, not feeling quite convinced. It becomes quite a cycle to steer yourself away from. Have I got this right? Am I wrong here? What exactly happened?

What did I do that was so wrong to that person? Am I going mad? These are very common thoughts to have and unless you have travelled that path it is hard to comprehend.

I had forgotten to block the email to this person and they contacted me again, they did not want to let go and must have been hurting a lot to behave this way. For gods sake just leave me alone and let there be peace.

Joe was taking his second year exams at uni around this time and he seemed to be coping well. I was proud of him more than ever for persevering when this had been such a tough year for him. He hadn't given up.

I decided that I needed to go away and specifically be by the sea for a few days. A few hours later I'd booked an air bnb down south near to Bournemouth, a place I'd got very fond memories of after going with Joe a few years before. I knew it and it was perfect when you don't drive. The train was booked and off I went at the end of the week. I was not as excited as I usually was at going away, these were different circumstances and I was listening to what my soul needed, I was looking forward to it though especially on the morning I travelled.

I sat chatting to the lady next to me on the train most of the journey to London, before we went our separate ways and I made my way through the early morning hustle and bustle of St Pancras. Two short tube journeys later and I was sat comfortably on the train Bournemouth bound. A coffee, a good book and my music for company and I drifted into day dream state for the next two hours. I had to laugh, the size and weight of my suitcase, you'd be forgiven for assuming I was going for four weeks not four days – never been a light packer! Anyway, on arrival at Bournemouth I decided on a taxi rather than haul this case around for a few hours, and asked to be dropped off at Boscombe Chine Gardens. The driver didn't know what I was talking about at first until I dropped the chine out of the equation. They are beautiful gardens and I remembered when I came with Joe last time, we had blazing hot weather and I did nothing but laugh my head off for the whole time we were there. As I stepped foot into the park, lugging my case on wheels for dear life behind me, I felt tears pricking and a few escaped from my eyes. I brushed them away hastily and took in the view as I slowly walked through the landscaped park and onto the sea front.

It was just as I remembered it but just a blustier version as the wind and sun combined shone down on me.

I'd been dying to visit the seafront café beach bar again and headed straight for that. There were people sitting inside but I wanted to be outside, it wasn't cold, just breezy.

I plonked myself onto a seat, looking out to sea and smelt the salty sea air. There's something just so magical about the sea, so cathartic and soothing and I bathed in that feeling. The sun came out further and felt rather warm and the waitress came out to take my order. Cuba Libra – double; my holiday drink. People from inside slowly came to sit outside also.

Pulling out my book, I had a couple of hours until I could check into my accommodation. I felt relaxed in the sun and took some photos to remind myself of this view. It was also a massive dream of mine to live by the sea, I had strong visions of me writing for hours at a time with the waves crashing a few metres away from me. I was going to live that dream over the next few days, as I had designs on writing the bulk part of this book.

28

Returning to Normality

It was a mixed few days being away. I loved being by the sea, and at first I nailed quite a lot of written content for this book. After 48 hours of being away alone however, I began to wobble inside. I think the combination of writing about my experiences (always powerful), the hurt and confusion I still felt and being alone with my thoughts reached a peak. After taking the Sunday, which was glorious sunshine, as time out to relax on the beach and strolling the seafront with reading and coffee stops thrown in for good measure, I suddenly was overcome with this alone feeling. You know it's nonsense when you feel that everyone else around you is with someone but you still feel it, that. I brushed it off, but it added onto the other pile of emotions building up.

Sunday lunch on the seafront was lovely later on in the day, and although I'm an introvert, I do like company too and am rather sociable when I'm feeling it and was longing by now for conversation, different to the one in my head. I went back to my air bnb and entertained myself with a film and a glass of wine. Monday rained, and was rather grey and gloomy; I felt gloomy as I walked down to the seafront pub with my laptop, prepared for a day of writing. There was hardly anyone around and between the sheets of rain against the cloudy sky, Boscombe had a completely different feel.

It's amazing what a blue sky and the appearance of the sun can make to a place and obviously my mood didn't help. I ordered a latte, struck up some conversation with the bar-person and then settled in a comfy seat looking out to sea while opening up my laptop. The words started to flow and writing about Joe made me a little teary but I was glad to be releasing it at the same time. Better out than in as they say. By late morning, I wanted to sob. This was about my recent incident, it was the anger I had pushed down resurfacing, I had a feeling this may happen while I was away from everyone. I knew I had anger to release but that was always difficult for me as it scared me, right back to when it did when I was in my bedroom as a teen as I always felt at fault and that I was a troublemaker, as this was the message I'd been given. It often became tears and would be why I used to cry so much as a teenager. I was livid, but pushed it all down inside. I reached the point of no return and quickly bundled together all of my belongings and made my way back up the seafront hill as quick as I could peering through a glaze of tears. It was such a relief to open the door to my little space and I collapsed on the chaise lounge and broke my heart sobbing. I needed to do this weeks ago. I cried for a few hours and panicked myself with thoughts that I was sinking low to the dangerous stages of needing outside help. I'd tried all of these remedies and nothing was shifting my feelings. Intuition told me it was repressed anger and that if I could feel my anger I could use that to strengthen myself and lift myself out of this hole I'd fallen into.

The tears kept falling and I texted my friend who is a counsellor and asked if we could talk. Within the hour we were chatting, me still teary, but I was almost instantly reassured to be told that yes I needed to sit with my feelings as I was and then I would move forward and that I needed to *"lick my wounds"* after the experience I'd had. That took the pressure off of me and I was much calmer after that. The next day was going home day, but not until much later, so I did manage to get some writing done, feeling more clarity, and still watching videos to grasp a greater understanding and free myself from its hold.

It was good to get home, not quite the writing sea break I'd envisioned but it had been a breakthrough that I was most grateful for, as I was desperate to get myself back to normal. I kept up high levels of self-care and found peace with visiting sound baths, massage, meditation and sleep. Gradually I felt myself returning to normal, as I detached from feeling it was all my fault. I was massively relieved and happy. Normality felt amazing! It wasn't just me either, as Joe remarked that this was the best he'd felt for a few months too, that was music to my ears. I had a gut feeling that the dark period was lifting and we were both emerging as stronger than ever with a bright future.

29

CEO Of Your Life

We'd been waiting for approval from the Samaritans charity to see if they would endorse the charity book project which would really help with the book reaching more people universally. It had been put on hold for a while but this would make a huge difference to the book's success and the aims we had. Sadly it was a no go. I was deeply disappointed but the show must go on.

The next few weeks passed by and the book was created and we actually went on to create an Amazon number one best-seller which was incredibly exciting for everyone involved, we had three sponsors for the book also to help with printing the book. I'll share the link for this book in later pages as if you are reading this book, you may well find interest in this Courage book also.

A couple more weeks down the line and I amazed myself by bouncing back with renewed passion and high spirits, more wounds healed and new beliefs created. I turned my attention to business again and to scaling up my business while keeping the true purpose intact. This was always intensely exciting for me and I began to manifest freely again, now this clutter had been cleared and space created. New beautiful clients showed up, radio and many PR opportunities, a new business collaboration and a brand new inspiring mentor appeared on my radar which I invested into.

Over the last few months, I had been starting to focus on business growth before I got drowned in the personal struggles which always impact your business in some way. If you are not feeling on top form it affects your results. One of the small changes I had made was to begin to outsource more in my business but also in my home life to free my time up to spend on business growth. One task was my ironing and it really made a difference for my energy levels with Joe also helping out with chores once he was home for the summer. In order to become the person I aspired to be, I needed to embody that person before. Would the CEO Sam of a highly successful business operation be ironing and cleaning? No she wouldn't. Would she be mowing lawns? Probably not.

Fears of money and feelings of lack tried to creep back in, but I was adamant I was having none of it. It was time to take the next big leap in my business journey and no fear was going to stop me. Become who you need to be first, like attracts like and I was preparing myself to take massive inspired action. I got into an excited state as I had some troubles sleeping for a while, which started when I was anxious. I began to feel my energy rising within and my thoughts were changing to where I needed them to be again, when I reflected back to just a few weeks ago and the quagmire of fear and distress I was in, it was quite remarkable to witness my own growth in such a short space of time. This demonstrates the power of our mind and how we are steering our way and holding the powerful wheel to direct us wherever we choose to travel to. Waking up each day feeling passion and purpose was just the best and I truly appreciated being here again. I loved what I did and who I supported and all of it held much meaning for me, sometimes it could move me to tears, good tears.

My story continues as it does for us all, and in just the last thirty months since the words of *"The Invisible Girl"* poured out from me I have grown through many more adversities which I found myself bursting to share with you in this book: bereavement, business lessons, supporting my son with his mental health crisis, empty nest syndrome, my own healing, bullying and then the beauty of manifestation, resilience and letting go.

The biggest challenge I ever had was in realising who I was, not labelled, who I really was, giving her permission to be herself and of letting go of everything that wasn't for my greatest self and to feel deserving of it all. I am delighted to say that I am well on my way and I am blessed with the life

I have created for myself, which all began with my thoughts, which produced emotions, which created the reality before me. Once you grasp this, you can truly get excited about the sheer enormity of the potential you have in this universe.

Other Books

The Invisible Girl: A Secret Life
https://amzn.to/2YXOHL4

Courage: Stories Of Darkness To Light
https://amzn.to/2YEwoz

Contact Info

Thank you for reading my story, if it touched your heart then I'd love to stay in touch...

Hang out with me here
https://www.facebook.com/TheInspiringWriter/

Or here:
https://www.instagram.com/memoir_mentor_and_ghostwriter/

And if you too feel you have a story deep inside of you to share with the world to help others then please contact me here to have a chat:
http://www.samanthahoughton.co.uk/contact/